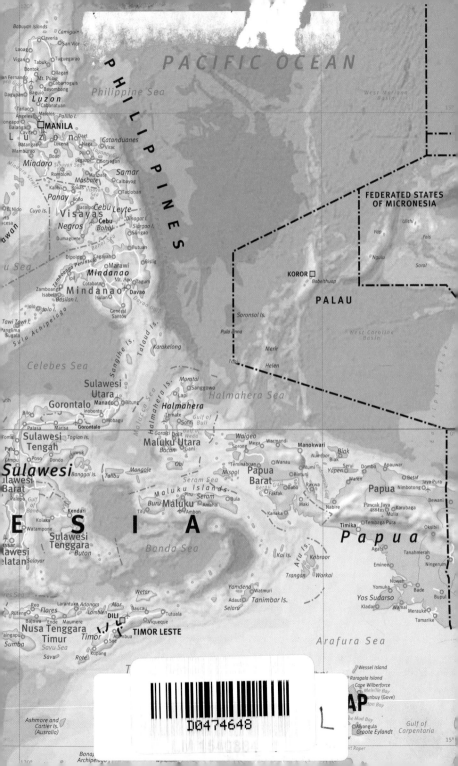

'The adventure of a lifetime' most aptly describes the 25-year journey of author **Linda Hoffman** in Indonesia. After 10 years in Jakarta, the country's heartbeat, and a brief stint in Bali, for the past 12 years she has been based in Yogyakarta, a university and historically significant town teeming with smart kids from across the archipelago, as well as tourists. Over the years, she has traveled throughout the country on public ferries, by horse-drawn carts, in cargo trucks and on foot to delve into the mysteries of the land and its peoples. With every discovery, she realizes there is still so much more to learn.

Published by Tuttle Publishing, an imprint of Periplus Editions (HK) Ltd.

www.tuttlepublishing.com

Copyright © 2013 Periplus Editions (HK) Ltd.

ISBN: 978-0-8048-4212-9

Distributed by

North America, Latin America & Europe
Tuttle Publishing
364 Innovation Drive
North Clarendon, VT 05759-9436 U.S.A.
Tel: 1 (802) 773-8930
Fax: 1 (802) 773-6993
info@tuttlepublishing.com
www.tuttlepublishing.com

Indonesia
PT Java Books Indonesia
Kawasan Industri Pulogadung
Jl. Rawa Gelam IV
No. 9, Jakarta 13930
Tel: (62 21) 4682 1088
Fax: (62 21) 461 0206
crm@periplus.co.id
www.periplus.com

Asia Pacific
Berkeley Books Pte. Ltd.
61 Tai Seng Avenue, #02-12
Singapore 534167
Tel: (65) 6280-1330
Fax: (65) 6280-6290
inquiries@periplus.com.sg
www.periplus.com

16 15 14 13   5 4 3 2 1

Printed in Singapore   1308CP

TUTTLE PUBLISHING® is a registered trademark of Tuttle Publishing, a division of Periplus Editions (HK) Ltd.

TUTTLE TRAVEL PACK

Indonesia

Linda Hoffman

TUTTLE Publishing

Tokyo | Rutland, Vermont | Singapore

ENTHRALLING INDONESIA

In many aspects Indonesia remains a wild and wooly place, beckoning travelers in individual ways, its sheer exoticism luring millions of tourists to its shores and into its hinterlands every year. Perhaps the least understood of Southeast Asia's holiday destinations, for many visitors Indonesia is Bali; for businessmen and women it is traffic-clogged, vibrant Jakarta; for zoologists it is jungles teeming with rare creatures; for outdoorsmen it is an endless array of activities; and for history buffs it is ancient monuments. While all of these are fascinating, each is only a tiny segment of the total picture. Regardless of what drew travelers to Indonesia in the first place, it is its charming people that most never forget.

Underlying everything—even the country's most visited destinations—are hidden meanings indicative of its myriad cultures and superstitions. Like a *wayang* shadow puppet play, what you see on the surface is what you're meant to see; for more understanding, you must dig deeper. A few lucky travelers become ensnared in this invisible charm and remain. I am one of them, and have spent the past quarter of a century traveling across this expansive archipelago absorbing as much of it as I can comprehend, excited by each new adventure and exhilarated at watching it evolve and take its place in the global arena.

This travel guide is a distillation of the country's most visited sites and pursuits, and it is designed to appeal to whatever brings adventurers to Indonesia. It covers a lot of territory in a small space; it is a shortcut, so to speak, to planning your journey and making every holiday moment count. It is my hope that once you begin your exploration into the 'real' Indonesia that you'll start planning your next trip back as soon as you leave.

Selamat jalan (Happy travels)

Linda Hoffman

CONTENTS

Indonesia **Overview**

Indonesians are among the planet's most heterogeneous people, their 300 or so different ethnic groups strewn throughout a string of thousands of islands roughly the length of California to Bermuda, making it an enigma that they are indeed one nation. Separated from one another by vast seas and the mountain ranges that form the spine of the archipelago, many groups have evolved independently of others, and their 700-odd distinctive languages and dialects, art forms and music lure ethnologists from throughout the world to study them.

Fourteen percent of the population lives below the national poverty level of US$22 a month. They have no running water or electricity and struggle with insufficient health care and education. Millions more hover near that line, yet a handful of the world's billionaires are Indonesians. In between, 42 percent of the population is now classified as middle class and, astonishingly, most of that growth has occurred in the last five years. This new generation of modern Indonesians is comprised of avid consumers and the fastest growing number of Facebook users in Southeast Asia, attracting corporations from far and wide to invest in the country in hopes of grabbing a slice of the lucrative pie.

Although the majority of Indonesians are moderate Muslims, there are also Buddhists, Confucians, Hindus and Christians and, in remote areas, those who still adhere to animistic beliefs. However, all the religions are enmeshed with ethnic traditions and superstitions. The existence of the supernatural is a widely accepted concept, and offerings to appease spirits are made in major cities as well as in small villages.

Indonesia's best-known landscapes are possibly the sculpted rice terraces on Bali and Java, any one of the country's 150 or so volatile volcanoes, expansive stretches of coastline beaches and its

vast jungles. But it also has a glacier-capped mountain in Papua, and in Nusa Tenggara, the eastern islands, endlessly stretching savannahs. In fact, practically everything about Indonesia is fabulously diverse except for the climate, which is generally tropical. But even then, temperatures vary according to altitude and time of year. During the wet season (roughly November to April), torrents of rainfall in short bursts are followed by smothering humidity in the western islands, while those in the east must content themselves with sporadic rains only one or two months during that time. In the dry season, humidity is lower but the sun can be blisteringly hot during the day and it is cooler at night.

Equally variegated is the plant and animal life here, with many of the country's exotic species of birds, reptiles, amphibians and mammals found nowhere else. Living in the forests of west Java are the last Javan rhinos. In Sumatra and Kalimantan, there are orangutans, proboscis monkeys, elephants and tapirs, with mudskippers and estuarine crocodiles floating in the rivers. In Sulawesi, there are unique macaques, dwarf buffaloes (*anoa*) and 'deer-pigs' (*babirusa*), while in Nusa Tenggara, Komodo dragons lurk. Papua houses marsupials such as tree kangaroos, marvelous birds of paradise and the large flightless cassowary, remnants of land links to Australia millions of years ago.

In the seemingly endless expanses of ocean on both sides of the equator that border its more than 17,000 islands are dramatic displays of marine life, ranging from migrating whales and dolphins to miniscule sea horses, with formerly unknown species being discovered every year. Indonesia was instrumental in establishing the Coral Triangle Initiative in 2007, a consortium of six nations dedicated to preserving what is believed to be the epicenter of all marine life, that ranges from Kalimantan to the Solomon Islands. It is also one of the founders of ASEAN (Association of Southeast Asian Nations) and is a member of the G-20 major economies.

Grand mosque, North Sumatra

Indonesia's
STORIED PAST

Batak tomb on Samosir
Island, North Sumatra

Gunung Kawi Temple, Bali

Indonesia's long and colorful history stretches as far back as 1.81 million years when Java was inhabited by humanoids, first by Solo Man (*Homo erectus soloensis*), followed by Java Man (*Homo erectus*) 150,000 years later. By 40,000 years ago, *Homo sapiens* had arrived and later, 18,000 years ago, a dwarf species, *Homo floresiensis*, dubbed 'The Hobbit', evolved in Flores. Fast-forwarding through separation of the land masses and human migrations, by the Dong Son Bronze Age (1000 BC–1 BC), at least some local kingdoms were already known outside their shores, as evidenced by the Moon of Pejeng in central Bali.

Hindu kingdoms were established in Java and Kalimantan by AD 400, and the archipelago was known throughout the maritime trade route for its aromatic woods and spices, which were traded for silks, pearls and other goods from China,

Africa and India. Sumatra's Buddhist kingdoms, circa AD 500, had diplomatic relations with China, which sent emissaries to Palembang to study Buddhism. One hundred years later, in the 7th century, the Hindu temples at Dieng Plateau were erected, followed in the 8th century by Sivaitic shrines at Gedung Songo, the Buddhist Borobudur temple, and the 9th-century Hindu temples in the Prambanan Plains, all in central Java.

Shortly thereafter, the center of power inexplicably shifted to east Java. Though little evidence of the ensuing three centuries remains, the archaeological site near Trowulan is believed to have been a magnificent city erected by the Hindu Majapahit dynasty (1293–1520), which ruled all of Java and into Sumatra, the Philippines and Vietnam, and had diplomatic relations with many other Southeast Asian countries. During the 1400s, the first Islamic kingdoms began taking hold, and by the time Majapahit fell the Islamic Demak kingdom had gained power, eventually forcing the Hindu aristocracy eastward into Bali and Lombok.

The well-kept trade secret of the origination of the precious spices that Europe paid exorbitant prices for via middlemen eventually reached the Western world, and in 1511 the Portuguese, whose forts still stand in Maluku, gained control of the all-important Malacca Straits. The Spaniards followed, and then the Dutch in 1596. With the formation of the Dutch East India Company (VOC) in 1602, Holland set about taking control of the lucrative spice trade in Indonesia, with headquarters in Batavia (Jakarta), where its 17th-century buildings form the nucleus of Old Town today.

Continually in conflict with local sultanates, in 1755 the Dutch neutralized

Terraced rice fields

Sasak lady and traditional weaving, Lombok

the last great Javanese Islamic kingdom, Mataram, by partitioning it into two courts. Located at Yogyakarta and Surakarta, the palaces of these two cities remain centers of Javanese court arts and culture even today.

In 1800, the bankrupt VOC was dissolved and Dutch colonization began. But while Holland was distracted by the Napoleonic Wars in Europe, Britain invaded Indonesia and ruled from 1811 to 1816. It was awarded back to Holland in the Treaty of Paris.

The early 1900s saw Indonesians prepared to die rather than to submit to further colonial rule, and a statue in Denpasar's Puputan Park commemorates one such sacrificial battle by the Balinese. It was to take another 45 years for Indonesia to declare independence but it did at last, at the end of World War II. It was another four years before the Netherlands recognized its liberation.

The new republic's first president of 21 years was followed by 32 years of iron-fisted rule by its second leader and a quick succession of three presidents thereafter. In 2004, the first direct presidential election was held, and today Indonesia has emerged as one of the world's strongest economies and a role model for democracy in a Muslim-majority nation.

Tuttle Travel Pack Indonesia
HOW TO USE THIS BOOK

Indonesia's mind-numbingly huge variety of choices in holiday destinations and activities can make deciding where to go first (or next) more than just a bit overwhelming. In this book, we simplify options by concisely listing the very best in several categories that this country offers to its visitors.

In the front of the book are two sections designed to give travelers a deeper appreciation and understanding of the country and its people and the sties they will see. 'Indonesia Overview' discusses cultures, religions, languages and geography. A brief time line of the past is covered in 'Indonesia's Storied Past'.

Chapter 1, 'Indonesia's 15 Must See Places', hones in on the country's top 15 tourist destinations, with insider tips on how to make the most of your visit. These sites were selected because they represent what Indonesia is to most people.

In Chapter 2, 'Exploring Indonesia', we have included these not-to-be-missed sites in itineraries. We show you what else can be done and seen in the same area in a one to five-day holiday time span (excluding travel time).

Chapter 3, 'Author's Recommendations', is a synopsis of the best accommodations, eateries, shopping, nightlife, spas, antiquities and kid-friendly activities in the regions covered by Chapters 1 and 2. But it also contains a section on Indonesia's best outdoor activities, hikes and eco-trips, some of which require more than the minimum one to five-day travel time.

Finally, vital travel information is covered in 'Travel Facts' to help you prepare for your visit before leaving home.

It goes without saying that many of Indonesia's other worthwhile sites and activities are not included in this guide due to limitations of space and travel time frames. Those options are topics for other books. By focusing on the best of the best, our goal for these pages is to narrow down the where to go, what to see decision-making process into manageable choices.

CHAPTER 1
INDONESIA'S
15 'Must See' Places

Sprawling Indonesia has so many wonders to behold that deciding where to go in a limited time frame is difficult. The top 15 destinations in this chapter are recommended because their infrastructures are better developed, meaning wider choices in transportation and services. After getting a feel for traveling Indonesian style, visitors will be prepared to venture out to more remote regions that require longer stays (see page 107 *Best Outdoor Activities* for suggestions).

ke Toba, Sumatra

cak dance, Bali

robudur, Central Java

1 Fatahillah Square, Jakarta

2 Jakarta's Freedom Square

3 Puncak Pass, West Java

4 Yogyakarta's Keraton

5 Borobudur Temple, Central Java

6 Mount Bromo, East Java

7 Petitenget, South Bali

8 Ubud Village, Central Bali

9 Bali's Bedugal Highlands

10 Lake Toba, North Sumatra

11 Bukit Tinggi, West Sumatra

12 Lombok's Gili Islands

13 Komodo National Park

14 Papua's Baliem Valley

15 Bunaken, North Sulawesi

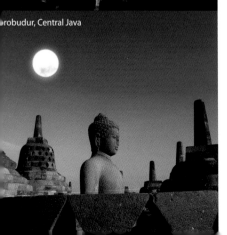

Making the Most of Your Visit

The most time-consuming effort when traveling in Indonesia is transportation: arranging it; waiting for departures by land, air or sea; and actually getting from one place to another. Especially if time is tight, highly recommended are the services of a reputable in-country travel agency that can shortcut some of this process, leaving more time for enjoying the experience of being here. See Chapter 2 for itineraries that include the **15 'Must See' Places** covered in this chapter.

A quick look at a **map** will speed up the orientation process. Six of Indonesia's most popular destinations are in Java which, generally speaking, is the best developed island. Several days could be spent in **Jakarta**, taking in its historic **Old Town** as well as its contemporary shopping, dining and entertainment options. From Jakarta, **Puncak** in west Java is within driving distance. Best done during the week so as to avoid heavy weekend traffic, there is enough to do in the area to take up an entire one to five-day holiday before heading back to Jakarta.

Yogyakarta ('Jogja') in central Java is the home of the **Sultan's Palace** (Keraton) and is also the primary starting point for **Borobudur**. There are several flights per day from Jakarta or Bali to Jogja and from some Asian cities. There are now several flights daily into Malang, accommodating **Mt Bromo** adventurers.

Two of Bali's hottest areas are **Petitenget** in the south and **Ubud** in Central Bali. The greatest density of resorts is in Southern Bali within a 30–60 minute drive from the international airport. Pemuteran and Seririt on the north coast and Candidasa and Amed in Eastern Bali require a few hours' drive from the airport over good highways.

Many Bali visitors opt to split their holidays between the southern beaches and charming Ubud, which can take two hours or more by car, depending on the number of stops at the handicraft villages along the way. From the airport, the **Bedugal Highlands** are reached by a road winding through spectacular countryside scenery and can also be done in a day trip from Ubud or north coast Lovina, if time is of the essence.

There are two of the 15 'Must See' sites in Sumatra. **Lake Toba** is entered through Medan, Sumatra's largest city. Its international airport services flights to other Indonesian and Asian cities. From Medan, it's a half-day drive to Lake Toba. The gateway to **Bukit Tinggi** is Padang, a much smaller town.

Lombok is Bali's closest neighbor to the east, and the options for getting to its shores include flights into its international airport and by sea from Bali by either public or high-speed ferry.

Reaching Nusa Tenggara (Southeastern Islands) is much easier than it has ever been before. **Komodo National Park** is reached via Labuan Bajo, in western Flores, where an overnight stay is required before taking a boat to Komodo Island the following morning. The regional airline that services Labuan Bajo stops in Lombok, thus for stays longer than one to five days, a Bali–Lombok–Komodo jaunt is possible.

Papua is a bit trickier. Regardless of your origination point, it's far from everywhere, but its remoteness has left the **Baliem Valley** ethnic cultures relatively unchanged by progress. Transit in Jayapura for flights to Wamena.

In Sulawesi, enter through Manado for an awesome diving experience in **Bunaken National Park**.

1 Fatahillah Square, Jakarta

Take a journey back in time to the Dutch colonial era

For a glimpse into the era when the Dutch ruled Indonesia, head to the Old Town or **Kota Tua** district of North Jakarta. Prior to the establishment of modern-day Jakarta, this area was called Batavia and was the central administrative center of the Dutch East India Company (VOC). Around the Old Town square, now called **Fatahillah Square** (Taman Fatahillah), are historic buildings in Dutch architectural style, several of which are now museums.

On the south side of the square is the neoclassical town hall built in 1712. Now the **Jakarta History Museum** (Museum Fatahillah), it was once occupied by the justice council that held shackled suspects in flooded underground dungeons. Among the museum's treasures are prehistoric tools and earthenware, weaponry, furniture, porcelain and paintings. In its archives are old maps and other memorabilia. A statue of Hermes, the god of fortune in Greek mythology, stands in the garden as the protector of traders. In front of the museum is a 16th-century Portuguese cannon, **Si Jagur**, its large fist regarded by many Javanese to be a fertility symbol.

The **Fine Art and Ceramic Museum** (Museum Seni Rupa dan Keramik), on the east side of the square, has endured many occupants, the most historic being the Dutch Hall of Justice. Constructed in 1870, it has also been a Dutch military barrack, the West Jakarta mayor's office and the city of Jakarta's museum and history office. Its superb collection includes rare porcelains, terracotta pottery dating from the 14th century, and ceramics from Europe and Asia circa 16th century. Its art gallery houses paintings by Indonesian artists over the last two centuries.

To the west of the square is the **Shadow Puppet Museum** (Museum Wayang) housing a large collection of puppets and masks from throughout Indonesia and other Asian countries. Built in the neo-Renaissance style in 1912, the exterior was renovated in 1938.

Wander behind the Shadow Puppet Museum to see the **Red House** (Toko Merah), typical of Batavia residences of yore. On weekends the square comes alive with street performers, snack sellers, sidewalk artists and vintage bicycle rentals.

Best Time to Go To avoid rush-hour traffic, go between 9 am and 4 pm. During the week, you'll practically have the museums, galleries and cafes all to yourself. **Getting There** Take a taxi and ask the driver to drop you at Taman Fatahillah. **Opening Times** Government-owned museums are open Tuesday–Sunday 9 am–3 pm, closed Mondays and holidays. **Admission Fees** Around Rp5,000 per person for each museum.

2 Jakarta's Freedom Square
Monas and other landmarks at the heart of the capital

In the heart of the often frenetic capital is **Freedom Square** (Medan Merdeka), one of Jakarta's too-few public green spaces. Crowded on weekends and holidays, it is all but empty during the week.

At the center of the park is **Monas** (Monumen Nasional), a towering obelisk capped by a bronze flame sheathed in 35 kg (77 lb) of gold commemorating Indonesian's independence from Dutch rule. A ride up an elevator to the observation deck reveals a panoramic view of the city, which is nothing short of awesome. In the basement is the **National History Museum** (Museum Sejarah Nasional) where, among rather simplistic exhibits and dioramas, visitors can hear Indonesia's first president, Sukarno, read the proclamation of independence in the Hall of Silence.

From Monas, it's a short walk to the **National Museum** (Museum Nasional) on the west side of the square. Indonesia's oldest museum, it contains an amazing collection of ceramics, stone statuary, prehistoric bronzeware, Chinese porcelain and other artifacts acquired by the Dutch. The bronze elephant statue in front of the museum was a gift from King Chulalongkorm of Siam upon its grand opening in 1868.

North of the museum are the **Presidential Palace** (Istana Merdeka) and the **State Palace** (Istana Negara). The State Palace, formerly the home of a late 18th-century Dutch businessman, is now used for important state functions and is not open to visitors. However, the Presidential Palace receives visitors on weekends unless the president is holding functions there. (Ask at your hotel front desk to confirm current opening times.) A guided tour of the mansion, built between 1873 and 1879, passes through selected rooms and outlying gardens.

On the northeast corner of Freedom Square is **Istiqlal Mosque** (Mesjid Istiqlal), reputed to be the largest Muslim house of worship in Southeast Asia. Officially opened in 1978, this enormous marble edifice stands on the site of the former Fort Noordwijk. Behind the mosque is the magnificent neo-Gothic **Jakarta Catholic Cathedral**, its black twin spires rising 60 m (197 ft) toward the heavens. A small museum on the second floor houses religious memorabilia. Staffed by volunteers, it is open Monday, Wednesday and Friday from 10 am to noon at no charge.

Best Time to Go To avoid rush-hour traffic, go between 9 am and 4 pm. During the week, you'll practically have the museums all to yourself.
Getting There The quickest way is to go by taxi to Monas. **Opening Times** Museums open Tues.–Sun. 9 am–3 pm, closed Mondays and holidays.
Admission Fees Below Rp5,000 per person.

3 Puncak Pass, West Java
Escape to the cool highlands overlooking Jakarta

West Java's **Puncak** resort area sprang to life at the beginning of the 19th century when a narrow, winding carriage track was built on the northern slope of Mt Pangrango to connect Bandung and Bogor, two important Dutch outposts. Its scenery and agreeable climate soon attracted visitors.

On the main road leading from Jakarta into the highlands, the star attraction in Cisarua is the **Safari Park** (Taman Safari), with an amusement park, animal shows, a petting zoo and food outlets in one section. In another area, visitors can walk or drive through a free-range wildlife area where exotic animals graze unfettered. Adjoining the Safari Park, the **Gunung Mas Tea Plantation** invites visitors to take factory tours to see young leaves being processed, and has guided walks or horseback rides through the fields to see the gardeners and pickers at work. For a bird's-eye view of the fantastic scenery far below, try **tandem paragliding** from high above Gunung Mas.

A bit further up the road is **Cibodas Botanical Garden** (Kebun Raya Cibodas), established in 1862, and a high-altitude branch of the botanical gardens at Bogor. Pools, flowing streams and great views of surrounding volcanos entice visitors to stroll through the grounds among its 6,000 specimens. Next to the garden's main gate is the principal entry to **Mt Gede-Pangrango National Park** (Taman Nasional Gunung Gede-Pangrango), a UNESCO World Network of Biospheres Reserve, and the home of many fauna species endemic to Java. There is an easy 90-minute walk to **Cibeureum Waterfall** and a more adventurous hike to the hot springs, passing colorful butterflies and birds, and probably many monkeys, en route. On the opposite side of the mountains at Bodogol are the **Bodogol Conservation Education** and **Javan Gibbon Centers** with hiking and canopy trails leading to **Cikaweni Waterfall**. Also in Cibodas is another of the country's five presidential palaces, **Istana Cipanas**, which is open to visitors.

Best Time to Go Go during the week for the best experience. On weekends and public holidays, the traffic from Jakarta to Puncak is jam-packed, eventually coming to a standstill that can last several hours.
Getting There A hired car with an English-speaking driver arranged through your hotel travel desk is the best way to go, giving you flexibility to stop where and when you like. The better hotels in Puncak can help your driver find overnight accommodations.

4 Yogyakarta's Keraton
Explore an 18th-century traditional Javanese palace

Designed and built between 1756 and 1790 by Sultan Hamengkubuwono I, the **Sultan's Palace** (Keraton) is a fine example of traditional Javanese court architecture, although European amenities were subsequently added. Every element of the Keraton is symbolic, and the compound itself is laid out based on ancient Hindu-Javanese concepts of the cosmos on a north–south axis that stretches from the Indian Ocean in the south to Mt Merapi to its north. The Keraton is the hub of the cosmos harmonizing the kingdom with the divine forces.

The best way to attempt an understanding of its many complexities, fraught with mysticism, is to tour with one of the docents here, many of whom are descendants of former royal court members or servants. A large wall at the entrance to the compound was designed to keep evil spirits out. Within, **Bangsal Sri Manganti Pavilion** (Pendopo) to the west is where the sultan receives guests, and dance performances are presented here on Sundays and Thursday mornings. To the east, the **Bangsal Trajumas Pavilion** (Pendopo) houses wedding palanquins, cosmetics tables and other treasures. A **European-style gazebo** with stained-glass panels was once used by palace

musicians. Dominating the courtyard is the **Bangsal Kencono Pavilion** (Pendopo), with a tall, peaked roof representing sacred Mt Meru at the center of the universe. Museums on the premises house royal regalia and sacred objects.

All are overseen by silent court retainers, men dressed in formal Javanese *lurik* (handwoven, striped) jackets and batik sarongs, while bare-shouldered, batik-swathed women are often seen in a procession en route to serving the sultan's thrice daily tea. After the palace is closed to visitors, these women also perform purification rituals with holy water and flowers to cleanse the Keraton from evil spirits that might have crept in.

Before leaving the area, have a look at the **Royal Carriage Museum** in the southwest corner between the main square (*alun-alun*) and the palace entrance to see many items made in Europe and presented to previous sultans by Dutch patrons.

Best Time to Go Visit as soon after opening time as possible as it closes early. Weekends and public holidays will be crowded. **Getting There** From Jalan Malioboro go on foot, by *andong* (horse cart) or *becak* (pedicab). Alternatively, hire a car, driver and English-speaking guide to take you around. **Opening Times** Sat.–Thurs. 8 am–2 pm; Fri. 8–11 am. **Admission Fees** Rp5,000 for foreign tourists.

5 Borobudur Temple, Central Java
Climb up the world's largest Buddhist monument

Three centuries before Cambodia's Angkor Wat was conceived, UNESCO World Heritage Site **Borobudur**, a temple, was constructed between AD 778 and AD 856 using millions of cubic feet of stone quarried locally. Rising from atop a sacred hill, pilgrims then, and now, circumambulated the galleries, moving upward from terrace to terrace, symbolizing Prince Siddhartha's journey to Nirvana. Each level represents a stage of the Mahayana Buddhist universe and is watched over by 432 **Buddha sculptures**, each displaying one of the five hand positions (*mudra*). **Miniature stupas** dot the upper levels, many of them containing meditating Buddha images. The 1,460 intricately carved **bas reliefs** depict Buddha's previous incarnations, life and teachings and include scenes from ancient Java daily life. In contrast to the lower tiers, the top level is open to the sky, representing Nirvana. A **massive stupa** in its center is the final stage of the journey.

The best way to attempt a glimmer of understanding of Borobudur's significance is by hiring one of the expert guides at the park, who speak several languages.

Within a century after its completion, Borobudur was abandoned, the reason for its desertion remaining an enigma. Thomas Stamford Raffles tried to reclaim it in the early 19th century but abandoned the project for fear of damaging its structure. Subsequent Dutch rescue attempts failed, then in 1975 a nine-year UNESCO restoration project took place, entailing the removal, repair and replacement of over a million stone blocks. Borobudur received another massive cleanup following the historic Mt Merapi eruption in October–November 2010. International and Indonesian experts painstakingly removed the volcanic ash that ensconced it and dismantled more than 55,000 stone blocks in order to access the drainage system that was clogged by silt.

Near the park's exit are two museums. The **Karmawibhangga Archaeology Museum** contains sculptures, stones and other elements from Borobudur. The **Ship Museum** (Samudra Raksa Museum Kapal) houses a wooden outrigger ship that was built based on images on the bas reliefs and sailed to Madagascar in 2003 to retrace the cinnamon trade route that existed at the time Borobudur was originally constructed.

Best Time to Go Get an early start to avoid the midday heat; sunrise is divine from the highest level. Weekends and public holidays are very crowded. **Getting There** Borobudur is 40 minutes north of Yogyakarta. Hire a car with English-speaking driver so you can stop along the way. **Opening Times** 6 am–5.30 pm. **Admission Fees** US$20 for foreign tourists. **Contact** http://borobudurpark.co.id

6 Mount Bromo, East Java
Spectacular moonscapes atop a huge volcanic crater

Situated in an ancient caldera, **Mt Bromo** (Gunung Bromo) is one of five peaks rising out of an otherworldly sand sea. With Java's tallest peak, active **Mt Semeru** (Gunung Semeru) (3,676 m/12,060 ft) looming in the distance, it is a spectacular display of nature at its eeriest.

The most commonly taken route to the summit begins with staying overnight in either **Ngadisari**, **Sukapura** or **Cemara Lawan** villages, rising at 2–3 am to begin the trek on foot or by pony. (Caution: Temperatures dip severely at night at this altitude, so take warm clothes, including hats and gloves.) Huddling against other pilgrims for warmth, climb the 250 steps to the crater rim in pitch darkness and wait patiently for the sun to appear. When the red, orange, yellow and purple sky reveals the rising sun and visitors are able to tear their eyes from the heavens, looking down they realize they are staring into the mountain's sulfur-belching crater. Foothold secure and able to look up again, there's a panoramic view of the entire caldera. To the west of Mt Bromo is **Mt Batok** (Gunung Batok), a perfect cone volcano with fluted ridges.

After trekking around the crater rim to behold nature in its full glory, you can take a prearranged jeep to the higher **Mt Penanjakan** (Gunung Penanjakan) (400 m/1,312 ft) for a bird's-eye view of Bromo from above.

This area is known as the **Tengger Highlands**, and on this land lives Java's only remaining predominately Hindu community, descendants of Indonesia's last Hindu–Buddhist empire, who fled to east Java in the 16th century to avoid Islamic invaders. While the dynasty's royalty and priests ended up in Bali and became the ancestors of those known today as the Bali Aga, the commoners fled to the Tengger Highlands. Each year the Tenggerese hold a tribal ritual called **Kasada**, tossing offerings of crops, livestock and other goods into Bromo's crater to pay respect to their ancestors in exchange for protection and fertile farmland.

Best Time to Go Dry season months (April–October). **Getting There** Fly to Malang, then go by hired car (3–4 hrs) or public bus to overnight near the volcano before making the pre-sunrise ascent the following day. **Admission Fees** Rp25,000 for foreign tourists. **Traveler's Tip** Bromo is an active volcano; its last eruption was in 2011. Check locally before going to be sure that it is inactive.

7 Petitenget, South Bali
Shop till you drop in Bali's trendiest beach resort

At the northern edge of southern Bali's trendy Seminyak is the even more elegant Petitenget, which is on the verge of making itself known as the island's chicest resort area.

The street that divides Seminyak and Petitenget has survived many identity transformations, from Jalan Oberoi to Jalan Laksmana and now **Jalan Kayu Aya**, but regardless of its current no-menclature, it is the heart of 'the' place to shop, wine, dine and stay. Among the almost unbelievable array of boutiques showcasing fashions for women and men, shoes, bags, accessories, home-wares and furniture, Paul Ropp's ethnic fashions, Bamboo Blond's funky dresses and Vinoti Living's interiors shine. Delectable dining choices, ranging from Asian to European cuisine, are omni-present, with La Lucciola's sunset cock-tails and Sunday brunches and Ku de Ta's 'it crowd' ambience nothing short of legendary.

Running north from Jalan Kayu Aya is **Jalan Petitenget**, once a quiet coun-try road and now a major street that extends luxury lifestyles further afield from the famed southern beaches. In stark contrast to the cheap souvenirs, budget food and accommodations and shirtless beach boys found there, new developments are catering to the young-at-heart ready to spend their hard-earned money on holiday-making. The **Potato Head Beach Club** is a fine example of the eclectic newness found along this road. Combining an art installation-style decor with pricey gourmet food and cocktails, it caters to

the uber contemporary fun-seeker and is drawing crowds. Likewise, the swanky **W Retreat & Spa** is a far cry from the basic homestays in Kuta. There are no problems finding food of every sort here, with Cuban food at **Cubana Bar & Grill** on one end of the scale of uniqueness and Pan-Asian cuisine at **The Living Room** among the choices. Absolutely positively not to be missed is the inno-vative cuisine at **Mozaic Beach Club**. And, of course, the fabled **Hu'u Bar** rocks at night.

Dress codes apply in many of Petitenget's restaurants, so leave your singlets and baggy pants at home and don your best resort wear.

Best Time to Go Early morning or late afternoon to avoid the midday sun. Walk until your feet beg you to stop, duck into a cafe for lunch, indulge in sun-downers on the beach and mingle with the jet set until dawn. **Getting There** The traffic in this area is horrendous. Wear your most comfy shoes and walk, walk, walk. **Opening Times** Shops are generally open 9 am–9 pm. Restaurants vary, with some open for breakfast and some beginning service at lunch.

8 Ubud Village, Central Bali
Eat, pray, love and shop—or simply sit and meditate

Tucked in the foothills of central Bali, Ubud is at the heart of several villages that have entranced visitors for decades with their magnificent scenery, artistic people, cultural and spiritual attributes, and more recently, some of the best spas and wellness centers in Indonesia.

At the main crossroads of central Ubud, the royal palace, **Puri Saren Agung**, stands majestically across from the **traditional market**. Scores of cafes, bookshops and souvenir stores line the main road, Jalan Raya Ubud.

Ubud's most recognizable side street, Jalan Monkey Forest, heads steeply southward from here to the protected **Monkey Forest** at its end. Although a sacred place to the Balinese, visitors are guaranteed a laugh or two from its mischievous primate residents. **Komaneka Gallery**, a collection of contemporary art, shares the Monkey Forest road with newer establishments, such as boutique hotels, Starbucks, designer shops and cafes. Past the Monkey Forest to the south is **ARMA Museum**, one of Ubud's finest art collections, which also hosts dance performances at night. For a taste treat extraordinaire, reserve a table for dinner at the nearby award-winning **Mozaic Restaurant Gastronomique**.

To the west are two more of Ubud's best art museums, the flamboyant **Blanco Renaissance Museum** and renowned Balinese art collector's **Neka Art Museum**. Thrill-seekers squeal with glee at the adrenaline and scenery while white-water rafting on the Ayung River nearby, which is also home to the exquisitely serene **Fivelements**, **Puri Ahimsa Healing Center**. Exclusive Sayan village hosts upmarket resorts such as the **Four Seasons Resort Bali at Sayan**, and the **Como Shambhala** further north.

Ubud's fame has brought with it modern-day woes, such as traffic jams, particularly in the high tourist season (June–August), so it's best to travel it on foot or by bicycle, if you're road-savvy. For further explorations, public mini-buses called *bemo* are a cheap and easy way to get around, or hire a car and driver through your hotel.

Best Time to Go To absorb Ubud's serenity, avoid heavily tourist traffic months (June–August and Christmas and New Year holidays). **Getting There** Jump in a fixed-price taxi at the airport on arrival or arrange a pick-up at the airport with your hotel. **Opening Times** Shops are generally open from 9 am to 9 pm; some cafes open for breakfast, but some start serving at lunchtime. **Admission Fees** Expect to pay nominal admission fees at museums.

9 Bali's Bedugal Highlands
Journey to the Balinese highlands for peace and serenity

Although **Pura Ulun Danu Bratan** is Bali's most frequently photographed temple, until recently only a few visitors chose to base themselves in the **Bedugal Highlands** for explorations around the island. In the past, the basic accommodations here were not appealing to many visitors, but with development whooshing throughout the island at lightning speed, that situation is changing.

Snuggled in the crater of an extinct volcano, waterskiing, parasailing, canoeing and fishing on placid **Lake Bratan** (Danau Bratan) are popular sports, seemingly out of place with the dramatic *pura* dedicated to the goddess of the lake projecting into the water. A path from here leads to the summit of **Mt Catur** (Gunung Catur) (2,096 m/6,877 ft), and en route are caves used by the Japanese during World War II. At the northeastern side of the lake is a trail leading up **Mt Mangu** (Gunung Mangu), with an ancient temple, **Pura Pucak**, and spectacular views of verdant tropical rainforests blanketing the slopes of the southern plains and surrounding mountains. The local market at **Candi-kuning** is filled with area-grown fresh flowers, fruits and vegetables, which are shipped to hotels and restaurants throughout Bali every morning at dawn.

North of Lake Bratan is **Handara Kosaido Country Club**, its fast 18-hole masterpiece golf course considered one of the best in Asia. West of the country club, at **Munduk**, surrounded by tea and coffee plantations, are **Buyan** and **Tamblingan twin lakes**, with ample trekking trails. North of the lakes is a series of breathtaking waterfalls, the most spectacular of which is **Gitgit Twin Waterfall**.

Heading south from Lake Bratan is the extensive **Bali Botanic Garden** (Kebun Raya Eka Karya Bali), conserving more than 2,000 montane plant species from throughout eastern Indonesia, its library and herbarium open to visitors. Also in the garden compound is **Bali Treetop Adventure Park**.

From a base in the Bedugal Highlands, explorations can be made to the north coast, the Kintamani Highlands in the east and fabulous scenic drives to the south.

Best Time to Go There are several trekking trails near the temple, so the dry season (April–October) is the best time to go. **Getting There** Take a taxi or hired car from anywhere on Bali. The Bedugal Highlands is 50 km (31 mi.) north of Denpasar and can be easily visited in a day trip from Ubud, Lovina or the southern beaches. **Opening Times** Tickets are sold from 7 am onwards and the temple is open 24/7. **Admission Fees** Rp10,000/adult; Rp5,000/child; parking Rp2,000.

10 Lake Toba, North Sumatra
The world's largest crater lake, home to Batak culture

The world's largest and deepest ancient caldera lake, with an island the size of Singapore in its center, **Lake Toba**'s (Danau Toba) breathtaking scenery is sufficient reason to visit, but being among the primarily Protestant, outspoken Batak people who make their homes here is an additional draw.

The crater was formed by a series of mighty eruptions, the last one occurring 75,000 or so years ago. Encircled by fragmented peaks of the ancient volcano, over time it filled with water, forming a lake. Samosir Island is the focal point of the Toba Batak, the largest of the Batak clans. Once known as animistic cannibals, today they are recognized for their tearjerking love songs, boisterous beer drinking, music and excellent chess skills.

Samosir Island, reachable by ferry from Parapat, is an excellent place for visitors to base themselves. There is a wide range of simple but comfortable accommodations on **Tuktuk**'s sandy beaches. The burial grounds of Batak clan kings is in **Tomok**, the largest being the sarcophagus of an early 19th-century raja that is hewn from a single block of stone. Nearby are traditional carved houses painted in the Batak holy colors of black, white and red.

Northwest of Tuktuk is **Ambarita**, where tribal councils were held in ancient times. Megalithic stone chairs and a table that have endured three centuries once witnessed the fate of condemned prisoners, who were decapitated, cooked and eaten by the raja. Further north is **Simanindo**, where the elaborately decorated house of Raja Sidauruk is now a museum that stands alongside a row of curved-roof Batak houses. There are more sarcophagi at **Suhisuhi**, **Hutaraja** and **Pansur Duggal**, 5 km (3.1 mi.) north of **Pangururan**, and there is a popular hot spring on the slopes of **Mt Pusuk Buhit**, where the first ruler, Si Raja Batak, is said to have descended from the heavens.

Best Time to Go Try to avoid the high tourist seasons (June–August and Christmas and New Year holidays). **Getting There** Fly into Medan, then go by hired car with English-speaking driver to Parapat (4 hrs). **Admission Fees** Expect to pay a small fee or donation at museums and burial sites.

11 Bukit Tinggi, West Sumatra
The seat of Minangkabau culture, where women rule

Bukit Tinggi (meaning 'High Hill') is in the center of one of three gorgeous valleys that comprise the Minang Highlands and is the cultural center of the Minangkabau people. Among Indonesia's friendliest ethnic groups, they are also known for their keen intelligence. Although less than one degree south of the equator, the town's cool climate, welcoming atmosphere and excellent panoramas tempt visitors to stay on longer than planned.

Bukit Tinggi is ideal for walking around. Overlooking its main square is an obviously Dutch-constructed clock tower, **Jam Gadang**, topped by a miniature Minang house. This is a good starting point for explorations, as it is visible from many parts of town. Nearby are two lively markets, **Pasar Atas** ('Upper Market') and **Pasar Bawah** ('Below Market'), stocked to the rafters with fruits, vegetables, plastic wares, snacks, souvenirs and other items. Bargaining is done for sport here, so smile and get into the spirit of the fun. Nearby **Jalan Ahmad Yani**, the 'main street', is lined with shops and restaurants. **Bedudal Cafe** is a good stop for Western and Indonesian food and also provides tourist information in English as well as arranging transportation or treks to nearby nature reserves.

The town originally sprang up around the Dutch **Fort de Kock** (Benteng de Kock), built in 1825. Only ruins remain, but from here there are breathtaking vistas of active **Mt Marapi** (Gunung Marapi), which looms over the town, and **Sianok Canyon** (Ngarai Sianok),

a sheer-walled tectonic rift that runs along the length of the island. Even better views of this natural wonder are seen from **Panorama Park** lookout point.

From Panorama Park, a path leads down into the canyon where there are Japanese-built World War II tunnels. Keep walking about one kilometer, cross a small bridge to the left and climb a long flight of stairs to reach **Koto Gadang**. This village is populated by smiths creating delicate silver filigree jewelry, such as earrings and pins, and miniature items such as Minang houses.

Taman Bundo Kanduang Museum, near Fort de Kock, is a restored 140-year-old traditional house (*rumah gadang*), displaying Minang artifacts.

Best Time to Go Avoid weekends and the high tourist seasons (June–August and Christmas and New Year holidays). **Getting There** Padang's International Airport services frequent flights from other Indonesian cities and from Singapore. At the taxi desk, pay a flat fee for the 2-hour ride to Bukit Tinggi over good roads. **Admission Fees** There is a small admission fee at Taman Bundo Kanduang Museum.

12 Lombok's Gili Islands
Tiny islands, great beaches and not a care in the world

The tiny Gili Islands off the northwest coast of Lombok were once popular only with budget travelers who spent their days diving, snorkeling or surfing in the crystal blue waters, toasting glorious sunsets with Bintang beer and partying hard every night. The charm and charisma of these barren islands without freshwater sources and motorized vehicles remains, but with the addition of a few higher-end resorts, at least one of which lures a different type of traveler.

Gili Trawangan is the largest of the three small islands and has the greatest proliferation of high-end resorts and villas, along with a wide range of lower-priced accommodations. **Nightlife** is centered on the east coast, and the party scene is easy to find by following the crowds.

There are several dive shops on Gili T, as it's fondly called, and some have branches on Gili Meno and Gili Air. All offer fun dive trips and specialize in PADI courses for beginners and advanced students. **Shark Point**, off the east coast, is a prime dive site, and **snorkeling** is good off the main beach. During the wet season (November–March), **surfing** is

spectacular off the south coast. Glass-bottom boats can be hired for trips around the islands, and local fishing boats always stand by to ferry passengers from one islet to the other.

Gili Meno, the middle and smallest island, has the best beaches of the three islands, is the least developed and continues to be a favorite for backpackers. Off the west coast, **Meno Wall** is favored by divers and is also good for snorkeling, as is the northwestern shore.

Moderately priced bungalows and budget hostels are abundant on **Gili Air**, where **Air Wall** is the dive spot of choice, snorkeling is good from the beach and there is a good surf break, **Playgili**, to the south.

Best Time to Go Since this is an outdoor adventure spot, it's definitely best to go in the dry season (April–October). **Getting There** Fly into Lombok International Airport and from there go by taxi to Bangsal (1 hr), then take a public or chartered boat to the islands. From Bali, take a boat or ferry directly to the Gili Islands. **Accommodations** All three islands have a wide price range in accommodations. Gili Trawangan is the party island and has the best selection, Gili Air is preferred by families, and backpackers still flock to Gili Meno.

13 Komodo National Park
See the huge Komodo dragons in their natural habitat

A UNESCO World Heritage Site, **Komodo National Park** (Taman Nasional Komodo) accommodates nearly 50,000 visitors annually.

Komodo Island is the more popular of the two sites that can be visited, and the adventure begins at **Loh Liang ranger station**. The search for the giant lizards stalking prey or sunning themselves is a 2-km (1.25-mi.) trek through dry savannah leading to **Banunggulung**, though the route may vary depending on where the creatures were last spotted. The birdlife here is astonishing. There are species of both Asian and Australian origin, including imperial pigeons, yellow-crested cockatoos, friarbirds and flowerpeckers. With luck, ground-dwelling orange-footed scrubfowl will be busily building their mounded nests.

Treks on **Rinca Island** (pronounced 'ren-cha') begin at **Loh Buaya ranger station** and there are two trekking paths, one leading through monsoon forest and the other up a ridge that has fantastic views of the sea below. Rinca has populations of wild buffaloes and feral horses which are not seen on Komodo.

It is best to begin the treks on either island early in the morning while the animals are still active. Being accompanied by a park ranger is required, and they are experts at tracking the beasts and protecting visitors from them. The dragons' tails and claws are lethal weapons and the nasty bacteria that are imbedded with bites from their serrated teeth can be fatal, so beware. Longer treks are available on both islands with prior arrangement, for example to

Poreng, **Sebita**, **Gunung Ara** or **Gunung Satalibo** on Komodo.

Afterward, take a dip, snorkel or dive in the unbelievably crystal clear waters off **Red Beach** (Pantai Merah) just outside the park's entrance on Komodo. Snorkeling is stupendous off the beach, but divers are advised to go with an experienced guide as strong currents in deeper waters can be catastrophic.

Best Time to Go The dry season in this area lasts for nearly 10 months, with January and February and occasionally March the only months to avoid. **Getting There** Three regional airlines fly from Bali to Labuan Bajo, the usual entry point (1.5 hrs), daily. From there, boat transfers to Komodo or Rinca can be arranged at your hotel or prearranged through tour operators or dive charters. **Admission Fees** Rp70,000 (conservation and entrance fees), plus Rp50,000 per photo camera and Rp150,000 per video camera, plus Rp50,000 per group guide fee. The pass is good for three days, usable on both islands. **Accommodations** Labuan Bajo has several types of accommodations, with more being built.

14 Papua's Baliem Valley
Travel back in time to the home of 'Stone Age' tribes

The 'Stone Age' ethnic groups of the breathtakingly beautiful **Baliem Valley** are protected by some of Indonesia's highest mountains, with verdant sweet potato fields crisscrossing valley floors. There are some mind-blowing sights to see on day trips by foot or car from Wamena as well as longer jaunts requiring overnight stays under the stars.

The **traditional market** in central Wamena is a 'don't miss'. Dani men and women gather here to sell not only their farm-raised produce but also the *noken* bags that the women wear suspended from their heads, the *koteka* penis gourds sported by men, bows and arrows used for hunting and stone axes. Drive or walk to nearby Wesaput to a **suspension footbridge** spanning a raging river to see how the people live on the other side.

Akima, north of Wamena, is home to a **mummified warrior** said to be hundreds of years old and is only one of several sacred mummies in this area. It's a bit of a tourist show but an excellent chance to take stunning photos of the friendly Akima men and women in their traditional attire.

Further north is Jiwika, a beautiful location due to the colorful wildflowers grown in the fields that are dried and sold. After a 45-minute uphill walk, you reach a **brine pool** to see the local women making salt by soaking banana stalks in the water and drying them. There's another mummy in Sumpaima in case you missed the one at Akima, and most tours include a Dani village **pig roast** in one of the villages nearby, which presents colorful photo opportunities.

Best Time to Go Dry season (April–October) as paths are washed out and rivers swell in the wet season. **Getting There** Garuda has a 6 hr 40 min flight from Jakarta-Jayapura. From there it's a 45-minute flight to Wamena. **Admission Fees** A traveling permit (*surat jalan*) is required in Papua and is usually arranged by your tour operator or accommodation. Bring a passport photocopy and two 4 x 6 cm photos. Away from the city you'll be asked for money for photographing traditional people and mummies. Your guide can advise on current rates.

15 Bunaken, North Sulawesi
Dive with sea creatures in an undersea paradise

Deep, clear waters with pleasant temperatures, steep drop-offs, shipwrecks and multitudes of colorful sea creatures have attracted divers to **Bunaken National Park** (Taman Nasional Bunaken) for many years. One of Indonesia's premier dive destinations, the infrastructure at Bunaken is well developed and most of its dive operators are heavily involved in marine conservation efforts.

Although all five islands within the national park boundaries have excellent dive sites, **Bunaken Island**, about an hour from the entry point at Manado by boat, has the largest concentration, with each side of the island surrounded by vertical walls housing a dizzying variety of species in schools thick enough to blur vision. There are also vertical walls off **Manado Tua** and **Siladen Islands**. Swift currents surrounding **Montehage**'s 'Barracuda Point' and the extreme depths at **Nain** make these sites advisable only for advanced divers. **Manado Bay** also has some mesmerizing dive spots, its sandy slopes making it a favorite of macro photographers. There is a shipwreck off the coast covered with colorful soft corals and an enormous number of fishes, nudibranchs and flatworms.

East of Manado via Bitung (a 90-minute drive), dive resorts are springing up like wildfire in the **Lembeh Strait**. The main attraction here is muck diving, getting up close and personal with the black sand sea floor in search of pygmy seahorses, hairy frogfish, mantis shrimp and the like. There are also some great shipwrecks in this area, as well as soft coral-covered slopes.

When selecting a dive operator, look for those that are members of the North Sulawesi Watersports Association and Green Fins conservation group. Most offer PADI courses as well as fun, safari and night dives; some can accommodate technical divers. If a topside activity is needed while equipment dries before heading for home, highly recommended are day trips into the scenic Minahasa Highlands or into the Tangkoko-Batuangus-Dua Saudara Nature Reserve (Cagar Alam Tangkoko-Batuangus-Dua Saudara) to see some of Sulawesi's odd and endemic critters.

Best Time to Go The dry season (April–October) is your best bet for good visibility when diving. **Getting There** Manado is the entry point and is well connected with major Indonesian cities (Jakarta to Manado is 3 hrs 20 min) and via Silk Air from Singapore 4 x/wk (flight time 3 hrs 40 min). From Manado, it's 45–60 minutes by boat, arranged by your resort. **Admission Fees** The Rp50,000 per day park entrance fee is usually added to your bill by the dive shop or resort that you book with. Check to be sure that you are charged correctly and that fees are paid to the national park office.

Pura Besakih, Bali

Underwater landmark

Komodo dragons

Batik making, Java

CHAPTER 2
EXPLORING INDONESIA

Terraced rice fields

The itineraries in this chapter cover Indonesia's most important travel destinations, and each area can be visited in one to five days, not including travel time. High seasons are June through August, Idul Fitri, Christmas and New Year. During public holidays and on weekends, the roads can be jammed, public spaces crowded and airlines and hotels fully booked. To enjoy the country at your leisure, schedule travel accordingly. Transportation options within Indonesia change frequently, making it a good idea to book internal flights and ground transportation through a reputable local travel agency either upon arrival or via the Internet.

EXPLORING

JAKARTA

Experience part of old and new Jakarta in two days

See Jakarta map on folded map.

Long before Jakarta sprang into global awareness as the capital of the world's fourth most populous nation and one of the world's largest economies, it was an important 15th-century spice trading port. Destined to endure centuries of wars between internal kingdoms and with foreigners intent on controlling the lucrative spice trade, it still survived.

Take a stroll through Old Town to see the remnants of 350 years of Dutch colonial rule. Or join the throngs of sophisticated urbanites in trendy air-conditioned shopping centers, cafes and restaurants that range from casual to fine dining. Although traffic jams clog city streets and basic infrastructure has yet to catch up with overwhelming growth, Jakarta is a vibrant metropolis that oozes excitement and energy. For its 9.5 million residents from across the archipelago, Jakarta is home.

Day 1: **North Jakarta**
Journey into Jakarta's colonial past

Start your day on foot on the north coast at **Sunda Kelapa harbor**, an important 15th-century trading outpost for a local kingdom. Still a working seaport, watch barefooted men load cargo bound for other ports onto scores of colorful wooden *pinisi* schooners.

At the entry to the port is **Harbormaster Tower** (Menara Syahbandar), a watchtower built by the VOC (Dutch East India Company) in 1839 as part of its bastion overlooking the harbor. If you like, you can climb eight flights of stairs to the top for an excellent overview of the surrounding area.

The nearby **Maritime Museum** (Museum Bahari) is in a restored VOC warehouse. Interesting to stroll through, it houses models as well as actual boats used across the archipelago, charts and other maritime memorabilia. In front of the museum is the only remaining section of the massive **city wall** that once ringed old Batavia, the VOC port town. Keep walking south to see the 17th-century drawbridge, **Jembatan Kota Intan**, formerly called the Chicken Market Bridge. It has been restored and no longer raises and lowers, but was once used to allow cargo boats to sail from the harbor into the Kali Besar River.

From here, it's just a short walk to **Old Town** (Kota Tua) (page 11). During the week, its museums are not crowded, but on weekends **Fatahillah Square** hums with activity. By now you'll be ready for a lunch break, and **Cafe Batavia**, right on the square, is an excellent choice for its varied menu and eclectic decor. Be sure to check out the rest rooms on the first floor, particularly the men's.

Southwest of Fatahillah Square are two other interesting museums. The **Bank Indonesia Museum** was originally a hospital, converted by the Dutch in 1828. Recently renovated, visitors take self-guided tours through several rooms technologically equipped to explain banking systems and how money is printed. A numismatic collection is housed in a safety deposit box area before entering the museum itself. Across from this building is **Museum Bank Mandiri**, built in 1929, showcasing a collection of old coins, ledgers, safes and other banking-related items.

South of Old Town is Jakarta's Chinatown. Called **Glodok**, it is typical of old Chinese settlements throughout the world: crowded, noisy and full of shophouses, hawkers, temples and other interesting architecture lining narrow streets off the main road. At every Chinese holiday, lion dances, special foods and general revelry spill out into the streets, making passing by difficult.

Two old temples, both near Jalan Kemanangan, survive from the colonial era and are interesting to wander through. **Jin De Yuan** (also called Kim Tek Ie in Hokkian and Vihara Dharma Bhakti locally) means 'Temple of Golden Wisdom' and dates back to 1650. It was razed to the ground during the Dutch massacre of the Chinese in 1740 but was rebuilt in 1755 by a Chinese sea captain. Notice the architectural features, window carvings featuring animals and water lilies, and dragons chasing a pearl on the roof. Next door is the temple's medical clinic, which assists the needy. Both Taoist, the other temple, **Da Shi Miao**, has similar features but is not as old.

Glodok's other highlight is electronic stores galore. On Jalan Hayam Wuruk is **Harco Glodok** and north of it on Jalan Pinangsia Raya is **Glodok Plaza**. If you can't find what you're looking for in one of these two malls dedicated entirely to electronics, keep walking around. There are plenty more shops in the area.

After touring Glodok, it's time to head out of the city center before the rush-hour traffic sets in. For overnight options, see pages 87–8. For dinner, choose one of the eateries recommended on page 95.

Jin De Yuan

Day 2: Central Jakarta
The city's bustling business center

After seeing the downtown Jakarta sights (page 12), there's one more stop to make before having lunch and spending the rest of the day shopping in air-conditioned comfort. **Pusat Barang Antik** ('Antique Row') along Jalan Surabaya in the elite Menteng residential area, is undoubtedly one of the most interesting flea markets you'll ever see. Lining one side of the street are kiosks selling everything from junk to treasures. A sign at one shop reads 'If you don't see the antique you're looking for, we can make it for you', thus buyers beware. Shop for replicas of Dutch lamps, vinyl LPs, Chinese ceramics, old jewelry and aged furniture. If you don't find something here to take home, you're not looking hard enough.

By now your feet will be begging for a break, so follow the traffic to the fountain that everyone loves to hate. Locally known as the **Hotel Indonesia Traffic Circle**, it is the location of choice for peaceful demonstrations of every sort, always colorful affairs. In the evenings, teenagers hang out here to watch the world zoom by. On the west side of the street are three of the

Grand Indonesia Shopping Town

city's finest shopping malls. Doubling as recreational and entertainment havens, they also contain some of the city's best eateries within their climate-controlled confines. Peruse the directory of restaurants in whichever one you choose first, and plan your next adventure while you relax over a nice meal.

Behind the Hotel Indonesia Kempinski that faces the fountain is **Grand Indonesia Shopping Town**, a gargantuan upscale mall. Wear your most comfortable walking shoes because this place is huge. Chanel bags, Prada shoes and an 11-screen Cineplex are among the finds here, and on the fourth level is a kids' play area with babysitters, and there are restaurants galore. For fresh fruit or a salad you create yourself to take away, stop in at Ranch Market in the basement.

For more shopping and people watching, across the side street is **Plaza Indonesia**, beneath the beautiful Grand Hyatt Hotel, which has a glorious buffet spread at lunchtime. There are two Indonesian designer boutiques on the third floor, House of Obin and Butik Iwan Tirta, and the divine Aksara bookstore, among shops selling branded items.

Connected by a skywalk to Plaza Indonesia is **fx Lifestyle X'nter**, adored by the young at heart for its entertainment options and shops. For handicrafts and batik, up the street to the north a 10-minute walk away on the opposite side is **Sarinah**, an emporium stocked with handicrafts made by Indonesian artisans.

As daylight fades into dusk, the city rocks with an astonishing choice of venues and music (see pages 101–2).

Time Required Each itinerary will take half a day or a whole day with a stop for lunch. **Best Time to Go** Weekdays between 9 am and 4 pm to avoid traffic hassles; weekends and holidays are very crowded. **Getting Around** Hire a car with an English-speaking driver through your hotel travel desk. The driver can drop you off for an hour or two and pick you up at a prearranged spot to move to your next destination.

EXPLORING
BOGOR & PUNCAK
Escape from the city's heat
to the cooler highlands

and evenings. Recommended is a stop in historic Bogor en route, to visit its world-renowned Botanical Garden.

Day 1: Bogor
A scenic town an hour south of Jakarta

Puncak Pass is an idyllic mountain retreat on weekdays when there are no crowds, with ample outdoor activities to suit all ages and levels of fitness. Go for at least a couple of days to breathe clean air and relax, and don't forget to take a jacket as it's chilly early mornings

Get an early start and stop in **Bogor** for half a day. Bogor is formerly the site of one of Java's earliest kingdoms, which later became a holiday retreat for the Dutch. Set in the scenic Parahyangan Highlands at the foot of Mt Salak, the temperature is cool and pleasant. The pride of the city is the **Bogor Botanical Gardens** (Kebun Raya Bogor), a re-search station established in 1817 and

Bogor Botanical Gardens

In the late afternoon, continue up to Puncak ('the summit'). Overnight at historic **Puncak Pass Resort** (www.puncakpassresort.com), with beautiful views of the valley below. Its restaurant is well known for its Dutch cuisine, so be sure and eat at least one meal here (page 95).

designed with the assistance of botanists from the famed Kew Gardens in London. With thousands of species laid out over 87 ha (1,203 acres), there are many plants here that are difficult to see outside their native habitats, and tree-shaded pathways invite visitors to linger. At the north end of the gardens is the stately **Bogor Presidential Palace** (Istana Bogor), formerly the country home of a Dutch governor-general. Sir Thomas Stamford Raffles lived here from 1811 to 1816 while ruling Java. The deer that populate the grounds were imported by the Dutch in 1808. The palace is open to visitors but requires a permit. If you would like to tour the interior, prearrange the permit with your hotel travel desk in Jakarta at least one working day before heading out to Bogor.

A good lunch stop is **Bogor Permai Bakery and Restaurant** (Jalan Jendral Sudirman No. 23), established in 1963, serving authentic Indonesian Peranakan food. Buy sweets and desserts in the bakery to take with you on your journey. If you have time, pay a visit to one of the few remaining *gamelan* **gong foundries** in Java (Jalan Pancasan No. 17), where barefooted blacksmiths hammer red-hot iron into the various components of *gamelan* orchestral ensembles. The instruments are assembled and placed on ornate wooden frames in another part of the factory.

Days 2 & 3: **Puncak Pass**
Cool volcanic highlands above Jakarta

Stroll through the **Cibodas Botanical Garden** (Kebun Raya Cibodas), the high-altitude branch of the Botanical Garden in Bogor (page 13). Originally a research station focusing on cinchona (quinine) and coffee, assembling montane and temperate flora from around the world was a herculean task when it

Cibeureum Waterfall

first opened in 1852. Though a bit smaller than its mother garden, its 60 ha (150 acres) of plants, streams and good views of the twin volcanoes that loom overhead, Mt Gede and Mt Pangrango, are enthralling.

The entrance to **Mt Gede-Pangrango National Park** (Taman Nasional Gede-Pangrango) is adjacent to the gardens, and is an excellent opportunity to spend some time in one of Java's last remaining rainforests and Indonesia's oldest park, declared in 1889. Pay the entrance fee and get a permit to enter the park at the Information Center, where you can also get a map. There's a rocky 90-minute walk to **Cibeureum Waterfall**, favored by butterfly- and bird-watchers, and a chance to spot some of the several primate species endemic to Java. More adventurous souls can trek to a higher

altitude to the hot spring whose sulfurous waters are good for the skin, according to the Sundanese people.

The next stop is historic **Cipanas Presidential Palace** (Istana Cipanas), which houses some of first president Sukarno's vast art collection and has outstanding gardens. Visitors are required to prearrange a permit, which your hotel in Puncak can do one day in advance. Also ask them to confirm opening times, as the palace is closed when the president is in residence. **Novus Puncak Resort & Spa** (www.novushotels.com) near the palace makes a good lunch stop, and you can linger afterwards for a **spa treatment** there or opt for a visit to the magnificent flower gardens at **Taman Bunga Nusantara** in Cipanas. Known throughout Indonesia for its sponsorship of elaborate floats in

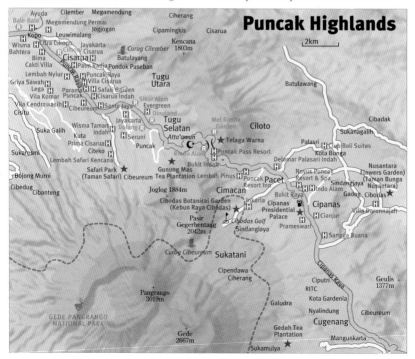

Tea plantation

the Tournament of Roses Parade on Thanksgiving Day in Pasadena, California, USA, there are many themed gardens representing various countries or a particular plant species. A guided tram ride through the park makes traversing its expansive grounds easy on the feet.

On the way back down the mountain toward Jakarta, spend the morning touring **Gunung Mas Tea Plantation** (Jalan Raya Puncak, Km 87, Cisarua) while the factory and pickers are active (pages 13, 112). The factory is closed on Mondays, but tours of the grounds are open daily. The workers have the day off on Sundays so you'll miss seeing them pick and tend the tea. One of the largest government-owned tea plantations in west Java, it was taken over from the Dutch in 1954. Obtain a map at the Visitor's Center and take the guided tour through the factory (30 minutes) to see how the leaves are dried, fermented, oxidized and sorted according to quality and color. Then walk through the scenic plantation on your own or take a guided tour on foot or horseback to see the pickers at work and the gardeners tending the plants.

Thrill-seekers can paraglide over the expansive tea plantation from the peaks above, which the Gunung Mas staff can arrange. The Tea Corner on the grounds sells snacks and tea as well as packaged tea for souvenirs.

At lunchtime, move on to the **Safari Park** (Taman Safari, Jalan Raya Puncak No. 601, Cisarua) (page 112), and have lunch at the **Rainforest Restaurant** while macaws, eagles and tamarins watch you dine. After lunch, check the posted schedules to determine what time educational animal shows are presented so you can pace yourself for the remainder of the afternoon. Also in the amusement park section there are kids' rides and permanent exhibits featuring Komodo dragons and hilarious Humboldt penguins, with new attractions frequently being added.

The Safari section of this conservation-oriented park houses animals such as lions, camels, hippos and orangutans, and you can take a guided tram ride, getting off and back on again at your leisure, drive through on your own, or go on foot.

If time is short, choose one of these half-day options and have lunch at **Cimory Resto** (Jalan Raya Puncak No. 435, Km 77) or its larger sister restaurant on the opposite side of the road. Both are outlets for a dairy farm nearby.

Time Required Minimum 3 days. **Best Time to Go** During the week to avoid traffic jams from and to Jakarta. **Getting Around** Hire a car with an English-speaking driver for the 3-day trip at your hotel's travel desk. Puncak hotels can help the driver find nearby overnight accommodations.

See Bandung map on folded map.

B andung can be reached by a scenic
but winding mountain road from
Puncak (page 13) or via the southeast
toll road from Jakarta. In the 1920s, it
was populated by well-to-do Dutch plant-
ers and merchants, its European-style
tree-lined boulevards and stately homes
meticulously designed by nostalgic
city planners. Today, its Art Deco architecture and factory outlet shopping are
major tourism draws.

Day 1: Bandung
Explore the west Javanese capital

B andung's Art Deco heritage is
evident in many buildings in the
old section of town. Start with three
hotels, **The Papandayan** on Jalan Gatot
Subroto, the **Savoy Homann Bidakara**
(Jalan Asia-Afrika No. 112) and the
Grand Preanger (Jalan Asia-Afrika
No. 116), all along one main road. Then
continue west to the circa 1895 **Freedom Building** (Gedung Merdeka, Jalan
Asia-Afrika No. 65), whose **Museum of
the Asian-African Conference** commemorates the April 1955 meeting of 29
Non-Aligned Movement countries striv-
ing for independence from colonial rule.

After spending time in the museum,
double back to **Jalan Braga** to head
north, stopping to walk around the street

once called 'The Paris of Java', where
caviar, champagne and European fashions were the order of the day. Today, the
cobblestone street is lined with heritage
buildings, cafes, art galleries and interesting shops galore. For lunch, stop at
Braga Permai Restaurant, formerly
Maison Bogerijen, which attracted
students by day and wealthy Europeans
dining on haute cuisine at night.

On the corner of Jalan Braga and Jalan
Naripan is the Art Deco **Bank Jabar**
(Jawa Barat or West Java Bank), constructed in 1936 by Albert Aalbers, establishing him as a prominent architect.
It was formerly the Dutch East Indies
Savings Bank and it remains in the
banking sector today. Continuing north
to tree-lined Jalan Merdeka is another
colonial financial institution, **Bank
Indonesia**, formerly Javasche Bank.

Further north, the **Satay Building**
(Gedung Sate) on Jalan Diponegoro was
named for the flagpole on top of the
central building, which is shaped like a
satay skewer. It was once the West Java
governor's office but today is used for
special functions. In front of the building is a large field that is packed on
weekends with folks enjoying performances, jogging or just hanging out. The
Geological Museum (Jalan Diponegoro

Satay Building (Gedung Sate)

Bandung Area

2km

to Subang

Lake Lembang
Sagala Herang
Sari Ater Hot Spring
Ciater
Cibeu
Nagrak
Mt. Tangkuban Perahu 2080M
Kawah Ratu (Volcano Crater)
Mt. Buleud 1207m
Carug Cibareubeuy
Karyawangi
Kawah Domas (Volcano Crater)
Mt. Kramat 1511m
Mt. Pamoyanan 1401m
Kertawangi
Mt. Masigit 1998m
Mt. Burangrang 2064m
Tea Plantation (Agro Tourism)
Mt. Lingkung 1529m
Mt. Kors 1430m
Bugbug Waterfall
Grafika Cikole Park
Cikole
Mt. Reungit 1449m
Cimahi Waterfall
Parongpong Park
Cikahuripan
Jayagiri
Junghuhn Park
Cikidang
Kertawangi
Sukajaya
Lembang
Wangun Harja
Pasirlangu
Tugumukti
Kol. Masturi
Mt. Masigit 1274
Kayu Ambon
Mt. Leutik 1176
Kol. Masturi
Boscha Observatorium
Mt. Cicalung 1203m
Ciboda
Pasirhalang
Jambudipa
Mt. Sereh 1226
Gudang Kahuripan
Cihanjuang Rahayu
Mt. Batu 1336m
Cikidang Fort
Maribaya Park
Pasirhalang
Katumiri Outbond
Langensari
Omas Waterfall
Pakuhaji
Panganten Waterfall
Padaasih
Cihideung Park
Cihideung
Wangunsari
Pagerwangi
Mekarwangi
Lélay Waterfall
Cihanjuang
Cigugur Girang
Puncrut
Ir. H. Juanda Forest Park
Mekar Mani
Cipageran
PARONGPONG
GH. Universal
CIDADAP
Ciburial
Mekar Saluyu
Cimenyan
Citeureup
Ciwaruga
Padma
Dago Waterfall
Dago Resort
Tanjakan Caringin
CIMAHI UTARA
UPI
Sukasari
Taman Budaya Jawa Barat
Marbella Suites
Mountain View Golf Course
Mandala Meka
Sariwangi
Karangsetra
Cimbuleuit
Sheraton
Dago Golf Club
CIMENYAN
Setiamanah
Cibabat
Sukajadi
Paris Van Java
Setiabudi Mall
Cibeunying
Cikadu
CIMAHI TENGAH
Pasirkaliki
Prof. Dr. Surya Sumantri
Grand Aquila
Siliwangi
Cipaganti Champelas
ITB
Juanda
Perjuangan Rakyat Jabar Monument
Padasuka
Sindanglay
Baros
Dr.Djundjunan
K.H.P H. Mustopa
Saung Angklung Udjo Ngalagena
to Jakarta
Leuwigajah
Cimindi
Raya Cibabat
Husein Sastranegara International Airport
Andir
Surapati
Geological Museum
Jend. A.H. Nasution
Leuwigajah
Andir
Bandung
Bank Indonesia
RE Martadinata
CICADAS
CIMAHI SELATAN
Cibeureum
Jend. Sudirman
Bank Jabar
Grand Preanger
Jalan Braga Historic Street
Jend.Ibrahim Adjie
Arcamanik Golf Course
Batujajar Timur
Melong
Utama
Freedom Bldg (Gedung Merdeka)
Asia Afrika
Papandayan
ARCAMANIK
Mt. Puncaksalam 904m
BANDUNG KULON
Pasirkoja
Savoy Homann Bidakara
Gatot Subroto
KIARACONDONG
Lagadar
Astanaanyar
Bandung Super Mall
to Cire Tasikma
Mt. Korehkotok 745m
Bojongloa Kaler
Peta
BKR
Buah Batu
LENGKONG
MARGA ASIH
BABAKAN CIPARAY
Jawa Barat Museum
REGOL
Soekarno-Hatta
MARGACINTA
Moch. Toha
BOJONGLOA KIDUL
Soekarno-Hatta
BANDUNG KIDUL
RANCASAR
Mt. Paseban 765m
MARGAHAYU
Padalarang-Cileunyi Toll Road
Sukapura
Cipagalo
Lengkong
Buahbatu
SOREANG
Cangkuang
DAYEUHKOLOT
Pasawahan
Citeureup
Raya Bojongsoang
to Cire Tasikma
Pameuntasan
Kopo Waterpark
BOJONGSOANG
Tegal Lu
Citarum Cataracs
to Ciwidey
Sukamenak
Sulaeman Airport
Bandung Indah Golf Course
Rancamanyar
Dayeuh Kolot

No. 57) is the next stop and although nothing about it resembles a modern museum it is interesting for amateur geologists and archaeologists for its replicas of 'Java Man' fossils, stones, a mammoth skeleton and other artifacts.

Before calling it a day, drive through the **Bandung Institute of Technology** (Institut Teknologi Bandung) to see fine examples of Indo-European architecture merging traditional Indonesian forms with modern Western technology. Dine at the nearby **Kampung Daun Culture Gallery & Cafe** (page 95) and stay over-night at the award-winning **Papandayan** (www.thepapandayan.com).

A trip to west Java is incomplete with-out a taste of Sundanese culture, so head back to town to **Saung Angklung Udjo** (Jalan Padasuka No. 119, www.angklung-udjo.co.id), a complex that includes a performing arts school and a workshop where *angklung* (Sundanese bamboo musical instruments) are made. Tour the facilities and join the 3.30–5.30 pm daily student performances of *tari topeng* (mask dances), *wayang golek* (wooden puppets) and an interactive *angklung* demonstration.

Day 2: Lembang & Tangkuban Prahu
A drive-in volcano above Bandung

To see what all the factory outlet shop-ping to-do is about and to view more Art Deco architecture, start on **Jalan Cihampelas**, also called 'Jeans Street', for outlandishly decorated shops selling all manner (and quality) of denim and other locally produced apparel. To the north, this street becomes Jalan Dokter Setiabudi, where one of Bandung's most

Limasan Villa, Jadul Village Resort & Spa

popular shops is located. **Rumah Mode Factory Outlet** (Jalan Dokter Setiabudi No. 41) carries branded clothes for all ages and both sexes, has a lovely garden, food outlets and clean toilets. At Jalan Dokter Setiabudi No. 229, drive by to see **Villa Isola**, once owned by a rich Italian businessman and now a university administration building.

Only about 30 minutes north of here, the environment changes dramatically as you pass hillside dairy farms and lush market gardens growing strawberries, vegetables and flowers. In Lembang, stop for lunch at **Jadul Village Resort & Spa** (Jalan Terusan Sersan Bajuri No. 45, Cihideung Bandung, www.jadulvillage.com), modeled after a traditional village. After lunch, get a bird's-eye view of an active volcano crater by driving to the summit of **Mt Tangkuban Prahu** (Gunung Tangkuban Prahu) to gaze down into its sulfurous maw. The result of a cataclysmic eruption thousands of years ago, Mt Tangkuban Prahu is only one of an array of dramatic volcanoes that ring the valley surrounding Bandung.

Time Required Minimum 2 days. **Best Time to Go** During the week to avoid crowds of tourists in Bandung. **Getting Around** In Jakarta, hire a car with an English-speaking driver for the 2-day trip at your hotel's travel desk . Bandung hotels can help the driver find nearby overnight accommodations.

EXPLORING JAVA'S WEST COAST
A fiery volcano, sandy beaches and a bit of history

Java's west coast is lined with beaches favored by weekenders and holiday-makers. Although the accommodations are less than luxurious, there are spectacular views of Mt Anak Krakatau (also spelled Krakatoa), the 'child' of the devastating 1883 volcanic eruption. Enquire about its status before planning a day trip there as it is still highly volatile.

Day 1: Banten to Carita
The drive to Java's scenic west coast

Before reaching the west coast, stop in Old Banten (Banten Lama), an ancient port town that was a major spice trading center as early as AD 1300 due to its proximity to the strategic Sunda Strait. Now a small fishing village, the most interesting sites include the **Grand Mosque** (Mesjid Agung) on the town square (*alun-alun*), with a five-tiered roof typical of early mosques in Java and a 16th-century minaret. There are excellent views of the town from the top of the minaret, reachable by a steep, winding staircase. On the east side of the square is a small **museum** containing historical and archaeological artifacts excavated at the site. One of Java's oldest **Chinese temples** (*klenteng*) is nearby and draws large crowds on the birthday of its principal deity, Kuan Yin, the goddess of mercy. To the south is the unusual minaret of a **Chinese mosque**.

If time permits, walk from Banten to one of two **bird sanctuaries**, Pulau Dua or Pamojan Besar, to see thousands of migratory birds that stop here, particularly between April and August, to take a breather en route to other localities (see pages 109–10).

As there's no good lunch stop in Banten, try some of the tasty local snacks to tide

Banten

you over until a late lunch on **Anyer beach** at Marbella Anyer. After lunch, continue on to **Carita beach** and spend the afternoon swimming, sailing, jet-skiing, diving or snorkeling. Overnight and dinner at **Carita Beach Hotel** (Jalan Raya Carita). Alternatively, book with **Java Sea Charters** (page 112), which can accommodate 10 people in four cabins, for diving, snorkeling, fishing and surfing. Their cruises also include trips to Krakatau and Ujung Kulon.

Days 2 & 3: Krakatau & Ujung Kulon
Take a walk on the wild side

In the early morning, take a boat across to ominous, smoking **Anak Krakatau** volcano. Boats to the volcano can be chartered on non-active days with a guide who will take you up the volcano's steep, sandy slope, but be forewarned that the trip to and fro is long and treacherous, particularly on windy days. After that, swim or snorkel nearby, with lunch supplied by your guide. In the afternoon, drive back to Jakarta. You can take the back road from here to Bogor to connect up with the Bogor and Puncak tour or return via the Jakarta toll road, bypassing Banten.

If you have an extra two days, continue on to **Ujung Kulon National Park** (Taman Nasional Ujung Kulon), a UNESCO World Heritage Site and home of the last surviving Javan rhinos. Don't expect to see one though, as they are highly elusive. The usual starting point for park forays is in **Labuan** to get a park entrance permit at the National Park (PHKA) office. From there it's a five-hour boat ride (not to be attempted in unseaworthy boats or in bad weather) to **Peucang Island**, where there

is an eatery and bungalows. Deer and large monitor lizards are common here, as are thieving macaques, so hold onto your gear. There is a large open field at **Cidaon**, a 10-minute sail from Peucang, where *banteng* cattle graze and feral Javan peacocks strut. Several other options for exploring the park are available, with one of the highlights being a canoe expedition up the Cigenter River on **Handeluleum Island** to journey into the heart of the jungle, carefully avoiding crocodiles and pythons. **Panatain** is the largest of the park's islands and is a good spot for snorkeling and fishing, as well as trekking into the rainforest in search of leopards, fishing cats, wild pigs and mesmerizing birdlife, including raucous hornbills and colorful Javan kingfishers. Javan Rhino Ecotour (www.krakatoatour.com) can arrange both Krakatau and Ujung Kulon tours. Guides within the park are required and are hired at the ranger station.

Anak Krakatau

Time Required 2–5 days. **Best Time to Go** During the week to avoid traffic jams and crowded beaches. **Getting Around** In Jakarta, hire a car with an English-speaking driver for the 2–5 day trip at your hotel's travel desk. Local hotels can help the driver find nearby overnight accommodations.

EXPLORING CENTRAL JAVA
Step back in time into the world of Javanese culture

See Yogyakarta Area map on folded map.

Base yourself in Yogyakarta (called Jogja by those who love it), Indonesia's second most-frequented destination after Bali. Travelers initially come here to visit Borobudur, Prambanan and the Sultan's Palace and to experience Javanese court culture but leave equally impressed with its citizens. A microcosm of Indonesia due to its high concentration of university students, it has a relaxed, welcoming feeling that reaches out to all who visit.

Day 1: Borobudur & Batik Shopping
Jogja's two main attractions

Most people begin their attempts at understanding the complexities of Javanese culture at **Borobudur** (page 15), starting early in the day before the sun gets hot and the park is crowded. By mid-morning it's time to head back towards Jogja, stopping first near Borobudur at the 8th-century Mahayana Buddhist **Mendut Temple** (Candi Mendut), which shelters three of Java's best preserved Buddha statues. The annual Waisak festival begins here, with thousands of devotees from throughout Asia following monks in procession after sundown to perform the ritual circumambulation around Borobudur.

Next stop is **H. Widayat Museum & Gallery** (Jalan Letnan Tukiyat, Mingkid, Magelang) near Borobodur. For a small admission charge, you can see some of the works of Indonesia's greatest painters and those of young artists and stroll through the sculpture garden. Off the main road back to Jogja, stop for lunch at **Jambon Resto** (Jalan Kebupaten, Ds. Trihanggo, Gamping, Sleman), where the fish you select is caught before your very eyes and cooked to order.

In the afternoon, go **batik shopping** at some of Jogja's finest boutiques. Choose between Afif Syakur Batik (Jalan Pendega Marta No. 37A), known through Indonesia for his exquisite designs, Gallery Batik Jawa (Mustakaweni Hotel, Jalan AM Sanghaji No. 72) for beautiful batiks made with natural dyes, or Ibu Hani's shop, Winotosastro Batik (Jalan Tirtodipuran), with some of the highest quality batiks in town. Better yet, visit all three.

Then continue on to **Kota Gede**, formerly inhabited by wealthy traders whose mansions have an interesting blend of Arab, Dutch and Javanese architecture. This is also the best place to buy fine silver filigree jewelry and ornaments, and many shops include tours to see the craftsmen at work. Have dinner at **Omah Dhuwur** (Jalan Mondorakan 252, Kota Gede) in one of the restored mansions. For overnight options, see pages 87–8.

Batik making

Day 2: Yogyakarta (Jogja)
Explore the palace and the old city

Visits to the **Sultan's Palace** (Keraton) should start early before it gets crowded (page 14). From there, walk south through the old city to the **Taman Sari 'Water Castle'**, a royal bathing pool complex designed by an 18th-century Portuguese architect. The castle is long

Taman Sari 'Water Castle'

gone except for a lone crumbling wall segment, and neighborhoods now encroach upon the once-glorious compound, but the eerie subterranean mosque, 'coiled' well and tunnels are still there. For a more vivid picture of how this opulent place was during its reign, hire a guide at the ticket booth and let him walk you through each structure pointing out its features. After the tour, the guide can point you toward the batik artists' shops in the village that engulfs Taman Sari. When hunger pangs strike, return to the rear of the Keraton and have lunch at **Bale Raos** inside the palace walls, dining on recipes that have been served to various sultans over the last century.

After lunch, start your foray into 'downtown' Jogja at the Keraton town square (*alun-alun*) and stroll up to **Jalan Malioboro** for souvenir shopping, passing several historic buildings. On the west side of the square is the **Grand Mosque** (Mesjid Agung), built in 1773, whose twin banyan trees are symbolic of balancing opposing forces. Further up the street are two lovely colonial buildings, now the **Central Post Office** and **Bank Negara**. Across the road, the old **Fort Vredeburg** is now a cultural center (Benteng Budaya), museum and exhibition venue (see www.jogjapages.com for schedules). Opposite is the **State Guest House**, originally constructed in 1823 as the Dutch resident's

mansion and rebuilt in 1869 after an earthquake leveled it. For a short while it was the Presidential Palace when Jogja was the capital of the new republic of Indonesia. **Pasar Beringharjo**, on the right side of the street, was built in 1925 and is Jogja's central market place. It is a crowded, intriguing conglomeration of kiosks selling everything from souvenirs to fresh fish. For dinner, try one of Jogja's most popular restaurants (see pages 95-6).

Day 3: South of Jogja
The mystical beach at Parangtritis

South of the town are the area's most sacred beaches. Closest to Jogja is **Parangtritis**, 28 km (17 mi.) away, rife with superstitions and myths, including that of Kangjeng Ratu Kidul, the goddess of the southern sea, who is said to have consorted with Javanese sultans in her undersea mansion. Hindus preform annual purification rituals (*melasti*) here ahead of their Day of Silence, Javanese pilgrims gather here to meditate on holy days, and the current Jogja sultan, a devout Muslim, still makes yearly offerings to the sea goddess according to ancient Javanese tradition with an elaborate procession from the Keraton in tow.

En route to Parangtritis are many villages, each specializing in a single **handicraft**, a fine opportunity to see the craftsmen at

Prambanan Temple

work and to do some shopping at wholesale prices (see pages 97–8). Have lunch of freshly caught fish that you select yourself, cooked to order, at **Depok** while overlooking the stormy sea. After lunch, relax and sunbathe on one of the more secluded beaches nearby (but no swimming due to strong undertows) or head back to town, continuing handicraft shopping along the way. On the outskirts of Jogja, in Tembi village, the **Tembi Cultural Center** (Rumah Budaya Tembi) (page 114) has an interesting museum of Javanese cultural items. Down the road, a good dining option is **d'Omah Hotel** (Jalan Parangtritis Km 8.5), a resort comprised entirely of beautifully decorated Javanese *joglo* houses. Every Sunday at 7.30 pm they have a *rijsttafel* dinner featuring 15 different Indonesian dishes.

Day 4: Prambanan & Surakarta (Solo)
Major sights to the east of Jogja

From Jogja, head east toward Surakarta (nicknamed 'Solo'), stopping to stroll among Indonesia's highest concentration of ancient sites at **Prambanan Plain**, a UNESCO World Heritage Site. The largest complex is the elegant Hindu **Roro Jonggrang** (also spelled Loro Jonggrang). Its main shrine, completed around AD 856, is dedicated to Siva, and it is flanked by smaller temples dedicated to Vishnu and Brahma. Beautifully carved and intricate bas reliefs depict narratives from the Hindu *Ramayana* epic, and alcoves shelter statues of major gods.

About 500 m (1,640 ft) to the north are two Buddhist complexes, Sewu and Plaosan. **Sewu Temple** (Candi Sewu) is older than Roro Jonggrang and consists of

a main sanctuary and over 200 subsidiary shrines arranged to generate harmony in the kingdom. It is believed that **Plaosan Temple** (Candi Plaosan) was built between AD 835 and 860 by the same Hindu king who constructed Hindu Roro Jonggrang for his Buddhist wife.

It's only one hour from Jogja to **Surakarta (Solo)** by car. Like Jogja, Solo is a court city originating when the Dutch, fearing the power of the Islamic Javanese Mataram kingdom, orchestrated wars that divided the court into two family groups. Although its heritage is not as well preserved as that of Jogja, its **Solo Palace** (Keraton Kasunanan) and museum is worth visiting for another piece of the Javanese court life puzzle. Solo is also a favored shopping destination for the goodies found at **Pasar Klewer batik market**, in front of the palace next to the Grand Mosque. For lunch, walk across the street to **Segar Ayam** (Jalan Secoyudan) for simple Javanese food and iced fruit drinks. After lunch, visit Solo's 'other' palace, **Mangkunegaran** (Puro Mangkunegaran) before it closes early afternoon. You'll have to double back to visit the **Pasar Triwindu** 'antique' market, a treasure trove of oddities. Return to Jogja for the night.

Time Required Minimum 4 days. **Best Time to Go** During the week to avoid traffic jams and crowds.
Getting Around Hire a car with an English-speaking driver at your hotel's travel desk.

EXPLORING SURABAYA
Indonesia's second largest city

Surabaya is a thriving commercial center and Indonesia's second largest city, with all the conveniences and woes that accompany a healthy economy. Throughout Indonesia it is known as the 'City of Heroes', thanks to its prominent role in gaining independence from Dutch colonial rule. Thankfully, a few of its heritage buildings remain.

The best place to begin tours of Surabaya, hands down, is **House of Sampoerna** (HOS, Jalan Taman Sampoerna, www.houseofsampoerna.com), which offers complimentary one-hour bus tours of historical sites on three different routes (Sundays and weekdays except Mondays, 9 am, 1 pm and 3 pm, advance reservations recommended) and a fourth tour on Saturdays. Take all the tours to cover the majority of city sights, and between departure times view the process of hand rolling Sampoerna clove cigarettes, visit the HOS museum, art gallery and gift shop, and have lunch at their cafe.

Most Surabaya heritage tours include the nearby **Red Bridge** (Jembatan Merah) at the heart of the city's 18th-century VOC business district. Always red, it was strategic in Surabaya's battle for independence in 1945. East of the bridge is Chinatown and Confucian **Hok An Kiong temple** (Jalan Slompretan), built by 18th-century Chinese merchants for the patron god of sailors.

Further south is the **Heroes Monument** (Tugu Pahlawan, Jalan Tembaan) commemorating the sacrifices of those who fell during the 1945 independence struggle. Next is the interesting **Cheng Hoo Mosque** on Jalan Gading. While primarily Chinese in design, features from Javanese traditional houses were incorporated when it was erected in 2002 to honor Admiral Cheng Ho, who converted to Islam upon joining the 14th-century Majapahit empire. The last drive-by is the circa 1794 **Grahadi State Building** (Jalan Gubernur Suryo), the country home of a Dutch businessman who was ousted by the VOC for corruption only three years later. In 1798, the Dutch governor-general took possession of the building and transformed it into a mansion, and after Indonesia gained its independence it was the home of the first East Java governor. It is now used for official functions.

End your day with a luxurious dinner and overnight at the historic **Majapahit Hotel** (www.hotel-majapahit.com) on Jalan Tunjungan, designed by one of the Armenian Sarkies brothers of Singapore's Raffles Hotel fame. It was also the site of the uprising in 1945 that sparked revolutionary fervor when student activists ripped off the blue lower portion of the Dutch flag and demanded independence from their colonists.

Time Required 1 day. **Best Time to Go** Avoid weekends and public holidays for a more enjoyable trip. **Getting Around** Hire a car with an English-speaking driver at your hotel's travel desk, or skip the car and take the House of Sampoerna free heritage bus tours.

House of Sampoerna

EXPLORING
MALANG & MT BROMO
East Java's ancient temples
and a spectacular volcano

Fortunately for Mt Bromo explorers, there is no longer a need to fly into Surabaya and go overland because now there are daily flights into Malang from Bali, Jakarta and other cities. A popular hill town during the Dutch era, Malang is still favored by weekenders and holiday-makers because of its cool temperatures and clean air.

Day 1: Malang
A charming east Javanese town

The Brantas River valley surrounding Malang city has been inhabited since at least AD 760, taking advantage of the vital trade and communications route that the river provided. Throughout

Candi Singosari

the valley are scores of antiquities with more being discovered each year (see pages 114–15). Serious Java history buffs will want to spend more than one day to visit as many of them as possible, but there are a few close to town for those who have only enough time for a quick look before continuing on to Mt Bromo (see Day 2 below).

Badut Temple (Candi Badut) is east Java's oldest monument, dating back to AD 760 but drastically altered during the 13th century. Now engulfed by Malang city, it is dedicated to Siva and is believed to have been constructed during the reign of King Gajayana. Southeast of Malang is **Kidal Temple** (Candi Kidal), built around 1260 and decorated with statues of the mythical Garuda bird on three sides. About 11 km (7 mi.) north of Kidal, **Jago Temple** (Candi Jago) was dedicated to a form of Tantric Buddhism and served as a funerary monument. It was built around 1280 and renovated in 1343.

Continue northeast to **Singosari Temple** (Candi Singosari). Another 13th-century funerary temple, this one honoring the last king of the Singosari dynasty. It has two huge guardian statues (*dwarapala*), indicating this temple was part of an impressive kingdom. Another 6 km (3.5 mi.) further on is **Sumberawan Temple** (Candi Sumberawan), a 13th- or 14th-century stupa, making it the only purely Buddhist temple in east Java.

Just a short drive to the east of Sumberawan Temple is **Purwodadi Botanic Gardens**, a branch of Bogor's famous Kebun Raya. The grounds sprawl across the lower slopes of Mt Arjuna and include the lovely **Baung Waterfall**.

After visiting the temples, return to Malang for lunch at charming **Toko Oen** (Jalan Basuki Rachmat No. 5). In the

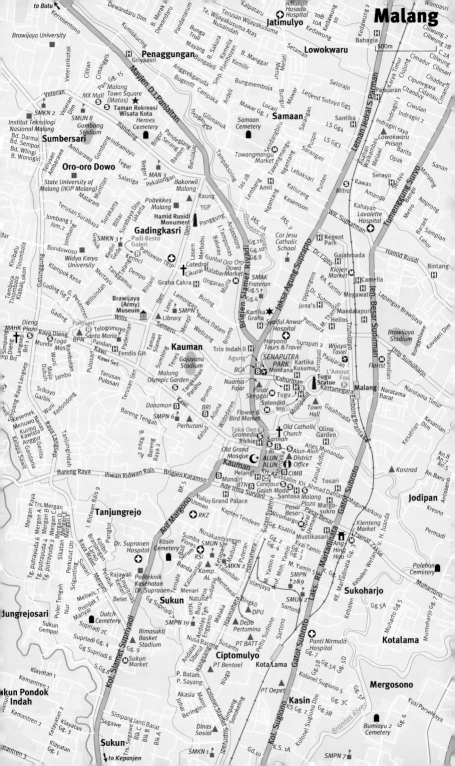

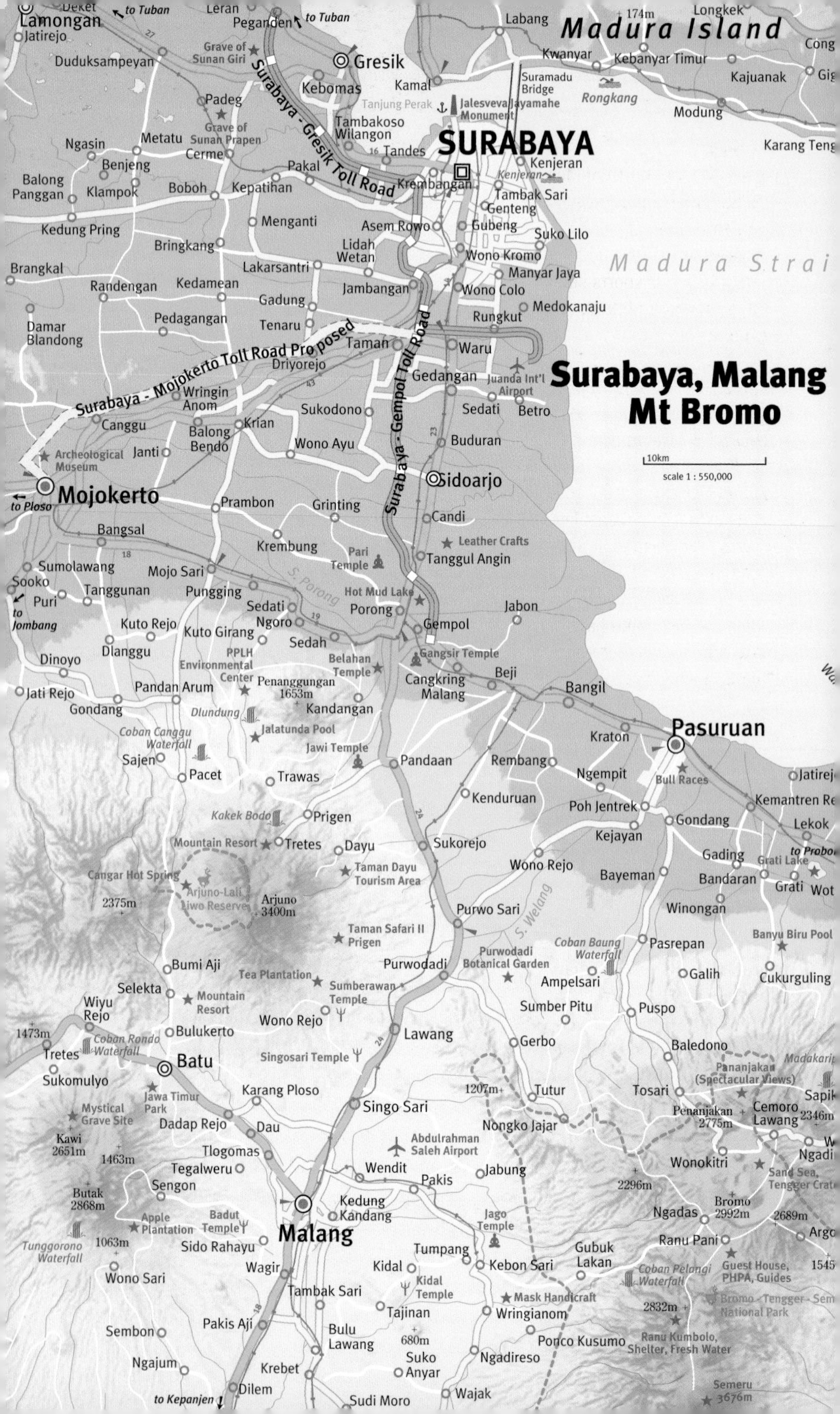

Surabaya, Malang Mt Bromo

scale 1 : 550,000

10km

Madura Island

Madura Strait

SURABAYA

Gresik

Mojokerto

Sidoarjo

Pasuruan

Batu

Malang

Bromo 2992m

Semeru 3676m

Bromo-Tengger-Semeru National Park

afternoon, drive up to scenic **Batu**, only 10 km (6.2 mi.) north of Malang, passing through apple and strawberry orchards. Another former Dutch hill station and now practically a suburb of Malang, Batu also offers adventure sports such as river rafting, mountain biking and seasonal paragliding. There is a giant statue of a reclining Buddha at the **Dhammadipa Arama Temple** at Junrejo, near Batu.

If time permits, take a stroll or hire a *becak* (bicycle pedicab) and go down **Ijen Boulevard** where many of the town's colonial buildings are located. Enquire locally if traditional east Javanese dances are being performed at **Senaputra Park** (Taman Rekreasi Senaputra) while you're there.

Stay overnight and have dinner at the **Tugu Hotel**, a museum-cum-hotel in Malang (www.tuguhotels.com).

Day 2: Mt Bromo
Java's most awesome sight

Mt Bromo

In order to reach **Mt Bromo** (page 16) from Malang for a pre-sunrise ascent, you'll have to leave the city in the wee hours to make the three-hour drive. Otherwise, you can go the night before and overnight at the foot of the volcano at **Java Banana Bromo Eco-Lodge** (Jalan Raya Bromo, Wonotoro, http://java-banana.com), focal point for the Mt Bromo Jazz Festival held annually in July. From there, join the pre-dawn procession to the crater rim on foot or by horseback. Take a jacket, scarf and gloves. It's cold up there. Coffee and tea vendors at the top of the mountain will be happy to sell you their wares, but you might want to take along your own bottled water and snacks.

If the trek across the eerie sands (about 2 km/1.2 mi.) and the climb up

250 steep steps in the dark are too much of a challenge, you can hire a jeep (Java Banana can arrange this) to drive you up to Penananjakan high above Mt Bromo's crater and wait there for a breathtaking view at sunrise.

Finish touring Bromo in the morning and pack up after lunch at Java Banana to head back to Malang in time for afternoon tea at Tugu Hotel. In the evening, join the fun at the Malang town square (*alun-alun*) where there are street vendors, impromptu performances and souvenirs for sale.

Time Required Minimum 2 days. **Best Time to Go** During the week to avoid traffic jams and crowds. **Getting Around** In Malang, hire a car with an English-speaking driver at your hotel's travel desk. Mt Bromo hotels can help the driver find nearby overnight accommodations.

EXPLORING
SOUTH & CENTRAL BALI
Asia's most famous
holiday destination

See South Bali map on folded map.

Bali's international renown primarily revolves around its famed southern beaches, surrounded by shops ranging from handicrafts kiosks to designer boutiques, homestays to five-star resorts, and budget to five-star eateries. Equally alluring, but in a different way, is the quiet hillside community of Ubud, which is home to painters and other artisans and health resorts.

Day 1: **At the Beach**
Tuban, Kuta, Legian and Seminyak

Spend the day at the beach of your choice, taking a break when the sun gets too hot to do some shopping. Each of Bali's southern beaches (see Kuta Area map on folded map) has a distinct person-ality, so selecting your base of operations is an important choice. Starting at the

first area north of the airport, **Tuban**'s mid-range and higher accommodations attract those who want to be near the action at Kuta but in a classier setting. The fun-filled **Waterbom** water park is here and it provides a day-long adventure for the whole family. The budget digs at **Kuta** are for those who will spend more beach and bar than room time. For raucous nightlife, point your dancing feet toward Kuta (see page 103). **Legian**'s guests are slightly older than Kuta's, but they still like to have fun, often spending their waking hours in Kuta but preferring to sleep where it's a bit quieter. There is a mind-boggling array of kiosks near these three beaches selling souvenirs, t-shirts and handicrafts and no shortage of food choices.

Seminyak, merging into **Petitenget** (page 17), are high-end resort and villa havens for the well-to-do, and their plethora of upscale restaurants and boutiques cater to the beautiful people (see page 98). Have lunch or Sunday brunch at the elegant **La Lucciola** on Seminyak beach.

At sunset, drive to **Pura Tanah Lot** (see page 115), which is beautiful at sun-set, but also very crowded. For a more cerebral experience, go early in the day. Have a superb dinner at **Ku De Ta** (www. kudeta.com) on Seminyak beach. For over-night options, see pages 89-90.

Kuta beach

Balinese barong dancers

Day 2: Jimbaran, Ulu-watu & Nusa Dua
A tour of Bali's southern Bukit area

Begin your day with a leisurely breakfast at one of the best breakfast buffets on the island at the **Four Seasons Resort-Jimbaran** in Jimbaran. After eating, drive down into Bali's southernmost peninsula, the Bukit, to stop at **Pura Luhur Uluwatu**, poised on a cliff above the Indian Ocean (see page 115). Be sure to hold onto your belongings, eyeglasses and shiny jewelry while touring the temple because there are herds of thieving monkeys here. Once they grab one of your treasures and leap out of reach, it's hard to make them let go. After touring the temple, take a moment to look over the cliff at the crashing waves below at one of Bali's hottest surfing areas. In the Uluwatu area are many of Bali's finest five-star properties, including the Bulgari Resort Bali.

After touring Pura Luhur Uluwatu, wind your way through the southern part of the arid, rocky plateau toward **Ungasan**, another luxury resort area and home to Banyan Tree Ungasan, before arriving at **Nusa Dua** on the east coast. A purpose-built resort compound, Nusa Dua's pricey Grand Hyatt Bali, Club Med, and several others, are populated with visitors who want a total tropical getaway experience with five-star amenities. In **Tanjung Benoa** further north, stop for a lunch of the island's best authentic Balinese cuisine at **Bumbu Bali Restaurant & Cooking School** (see page 96). Spend the afternoon enjoying every imaginable sort of watersport at Benoa or a spa treatment at any of the luxury resorts (see pages 89–90). For dinner, have freshly caught fish cooked to your specifications at any of the seafood restaurants lining Jimbaran beach.

Day 3: Visiting Ubud
A trip to Bali's artistic heartland

Long appreciated for its culture, handi-crafts and art, hillside **Ubud** (page 18; see also Central Bali map on folded map) continues to beckon, and its *kecak* monkey and *legong* court dances still mesmerize. Its charm begins with its cool mountain climate surrounded by scenic terraced rice fields and serene local folk.

The drive to Ubud is, in fact, a prelude to its artistic ambience. Immediately after leaving the main highway and beginning the ascent into the hills are artisan villages, each specializing in a particular art form. At **Batubulan** are stone carvers long respected for their temple facades and statues as well as their *barong* dance troupes. Next is **Celuk**, where silversmith and jewelry shops line both sides of the road. **Singapadu** is home to several respected mask makers and *gamelan* players, and **Sukawati**, an ancient court town, produces some of Bali's finest puppet masters (*dalang*). **Batuan** has been an artist and crafts village for over 1,000 years, its unique painting style exhibited in the town's many galleries. Wood carvers creating statues, furniture and masks flourish in **Mas**, and **Peliatan** is renowned for its *legong* dancers. Stop at one or more of these villages if you have the time and energy en route to Ubud.

In the afternoon, tour Ubud's best **art museums**, stopping to peek inside any of

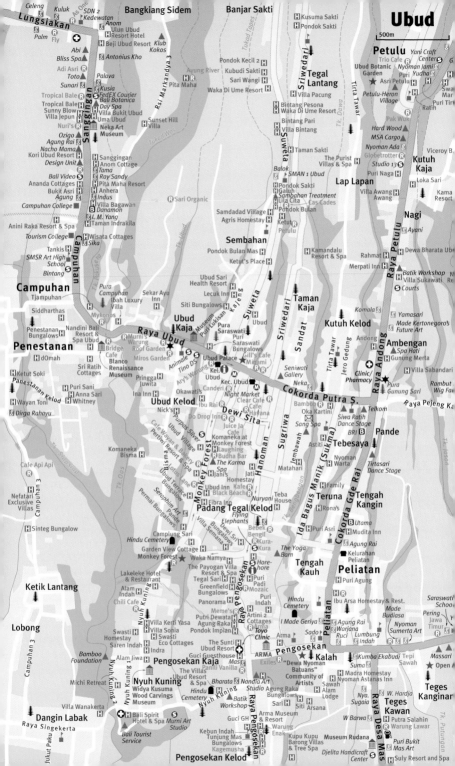

its many boutiques that catch your eye (see pages 99–100). **Neka Art Museum** (Jalan Raya Campuan, www.museumneka. com) has five galleries housing Neka's private collection by Bali's most revered artists. **Blanco Renaissance Museum** (Jalan Raya Campuan, www.blancomuseumcom) features Antonio Blanco's risqué paintings. On Jalan Raya Ubud is **Museum Puri Lukisan** (www.mpi-ubud. com), representing the evolution of modern Balinese painting. Further south, **ARMA** (Jalan Bima, www.armamuseum.com) (page 18) is Agung Rai's personal collection with rotating exhibits, performances and workshops, and to the east, **Museum Rudana** (Jalan Cok Rai Pudak, www. museumrudana.com) exhibits contemporary Indonesian and commercial fine art.

For lunch and dinner options, see page 96. If planning a dinner at award-winning **Mozaic Restaurant Gastronomique** during your Ubud stay, make reservations in advance. For overnight options, see pages 90–91.

Day 4: **Around Ubud**
Antiquities and spectacular scenery

Hire a car with an English-speaking driver or guide and take a cultural expedition, beginning with the **Elephant Cave** (Goa Gajah) 2 km (1.2 mi.) east of Ubud. Not discovered until 1923, it likely dates from the 11th century and was used by both Buddhist and Hindu pilgrims. The next stop is two important temples in Pejeng. The Hindu **Pura Pusering Jagat** (Navel of the World Temple) dates from the 14th century, and although its statues adorned with dancing demons grouped around a *lingga* are quite interesting, the most important relic is a stone vessel decorated with scenes from the *Mahabharata*

epic. Up the road is **Pura Penataren Sasih**, which houses a rare, large bronze kettledrum dubbed 'Moon of Pejeng'. Although kettledrums originated in Vietnam during the Bronze Age, a mold and several other drums have been found throughout eastern Indonesia, indicating that they were made locally, making their age difficult to confirm.

Your guide will suggest a good place to stop for lunch, and if a coffee break is in order, on the road from Pejeng to Tampaksiring, in Banjar Seribatu, is **Buana Amertha Sari Coffee Farm**, which offers free samples of plain, lemon and ginger tea, as well as plain coffee, coffee *luwak* and hot cocoa, all grown and processed on the premises. If time permits, you can take a guided stroll through the grounds.

Gunung Kawi ('The Mountain of the Poet'), near Tampaksiring, is a complex of rock-hewn monuments dating from the late 11th century that are connected with the youngest son of the powerful east Javanese King Airlangga, who was of Balinese descent via his father Udayna. Next to the monuments is a rock-cut monastery complex consisting of several caves with a free-standing building hewn out of the rock in the center. The last stop is **Tirta Empul**, one of Bali's most sacred places. A sanctuary of bathing pools connected by a courtyard, there are 15 spouts fed by spring water, which are used by devoted Balinese for purification rituals.

Bidding farewell to a select few of central Bali's antiquities, head back to Ubud. For nighttime entertainment there, see page 103.

Time Required Minimum 4 days. **Best Time to Go** Avoid the wet season (November–March), if possible, for a more enjoyable holiday, but beware of crowds during summer months (June–August). **Getting Around** For touring, hire a car with an English-speaking driver through the travel desk at your hotel.

EXPLORING
NORTH BALI
Travel across the mountains to Bali's quiet northern shore

See Bali map on folded map.

The Bedugal Highlands and Lovina both make excellent bases for exploring the 'other' Bali away from the crowded beaches in the south and from growing traffic congestion surrounding Ubud. Opt for cool mountain air and gorgeous scenery in the highlands or the beach scene on the north coast. Both are great choices.

Explorations into the **Bedugal Highlands** (page 19) for unbelievable scenery and cool mountain climes can also be made in a day trip from a base in Lovina on Bali's north shore. It can get chilly in the highlands, so take a sweater. Have lunch at **Ngiring Ngewedang Villa**

(http://ngiringngewedang.com) set in a coffee plantation overlooking the twin lakes, then return to Lovina. Overnight at **Puri Bagus Villa Resort** (www.puribagus.net). Have dinner at **The Damai** (http://damai-lovina.com), an award-winning restaurant that serves organic vegetables from its own gardens and rabbit and duck from its farm.

The area known as **Lovina** is actually a 12 km (8 mi.) stretch of black sand beach passing through six villages with different names. **Kalibukbuk** is at its center and has the highest concentration of amenities, but eateries, souvenir shops and a full range of accommodations line both sides of the main road that passes through the area. Kalibukbuk is easily recognizable by its dolphin statue standing near the sea, acknowledging one of Lovina's prime attractions, sunrise dolphin spotting. The younger set tends to settle in this area in one of the many budget homestays or the cheaper rooms in one of the multistory hotels. The further you get away from Kalibukbuk, toward Temukus village at the west end or at Pemaron in the east, the quieter it is.

Dolphin-watching at Lovina

Spend the day swimming in the calm sea, which is protected by coral reefs that block the dangerous undertows so prevalent in the south. Snorkeling is good near the reef, and colorful local fishing boats (*perahu*) can be hired for these excursions. The sunsets at Lovina are particularly spectacular. For lunch on or near the beach, follow the crowds to find the current most popular cafe or *warung* (small eatery), many of which are at Kalibukbuk on Jalan Binaria (Dolphin Street), Jalan Pantai and Jalan Rambutan. If an extra activity is called for, Warung Bambu in Pemoran, near Puri Bagus Villa Resort on the road to Singaraja, hosts cooking classes. For dinner, Lovina's **Adirama Beach Restaurant** (www.adiramabeachhotel. com) has an interesting menu with a variety of cuisines and a small wine list.

Time Required Minimum 2 days. **Best Time to Go** During the week to avoid crowds. **Getting Around** Check to see if your accommodation arranges transportation to Lovina; if not, hire a fixed-price taxi from the taxi counter at the Bali Airport (about 2½ hours) or arrange a car with your hotel in Ubud (about 2 hours). For Bedugal Highlands jaunts, hire a car with an English-speaking driver through your hotel's travel desk.

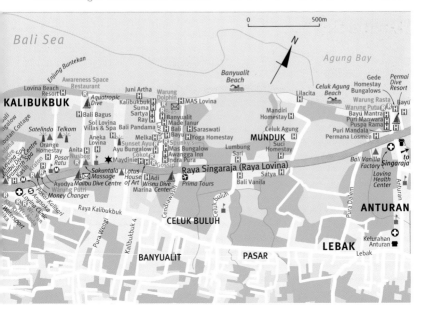

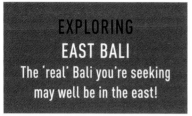

EXPLORING EAST BALI
The 'real' Bali you're seeking may well be in the east!

See Bali map on folded map.

Floating Pavilion (Balé Kambang)

Base yourself in either Candidasa or Amed for snorkeling and diving and for cultural trips inland. In either location, check the tide schedules before planning your day. When the tide is out, go touring, saving the beach for the other half of the day. All hotels are connected to dive shops that can help plan your underwater adventures.

Day 1: Semarapura to Kamasan & Candidasa
Land of ancient kingdoms

En route to eastern Bali, stop at Semarapura (formerly called

Klungkung), a small town that might have been forgotten except for the unique antiquities at its very heart. Although nothing but a great gate remains of the old palace, Puri Semarapura ('Palace of the God of Love'), the two buildings that still stand, the **Kertha Gosa Hall of Justice** and the larger **Floating Pavilion** (Balé Kambang) next to it, are decorated with Kamasan *wayang*-style paintings that have to be seen to be believed. As the

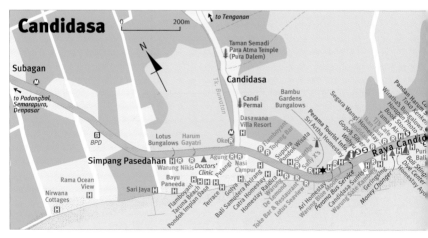

Candidasa

0   200m

N

to Tenganan

Subagan

to Padangbai, Semarapura, Denpasar

Taman Semadi
Para Atma Temple
(Pura Dalem)

Candidasa

Candi Permai

Bambu Gardens Bungalows

Dasawana Villa Resort

BPD

Lotus Bungalows

Harum Gayatri

Oke

Perama Tourist Info

Sri Artha Homestay

Pondok Wisata

Topeng Bar

Flamboyant

Sutra

Sally X's

Pandan Harum

Wiratha's Bungalows

Toko Teenek

Hangan Store

Boni Store

TJ's Café

Ikan Laut

Taman Air

Candi Gogok Silver

Raya Candid

Puri

Bali Santi

Dive Center

Homestay Ayu

Simpang Pasedahan

Warung Nikis

Doctors' Clinic

Agung

Nasi Campur

Bayu Paneeda

Sari Jaya

Flamboyan

Tatuna Beach

Pondok Implan Desa

Terrace

Golya

Catra Homestay

Bali Samudera

Arirang

Homestay Radio

De Lemond

Toke Bar & Restaurant

Lotus Seaview

Ari Homestay

Warung Blue Moon

Candidasa Sunrise

Warung Sate Kambing

Perama Bus Service

Money Changer

Rama Ocean View

Nirwana Cottages

name implies, the Hall of Justice was used by great Klungkung kings, who once ruled all of Bali, to dispense punishments on wrongdoers. The paintings on the ceilings of both buildings depict the fates awaiting those who are evil in hell and of the delights of the gods in heaven. Although the paintings have been repaired several times by talented artists over the years, only an expert would be able to differentiate the restored pieces from the originals.

If you have time, visit **Kamasan village**, less than 5 km (3 mi.) away, an artistic center that is home not only to painters but to silversmiths and puppeteers (*dalang*) as well. Several workshops are open to the public to see the artisans at work, and of course for shopping.

There's not a really great place to eat in this area, so proceed to **Candidasa** and dive into one of the best burgers in Bali at **Ari Homestay & Hot Dog Shop** on Jalan Raya Candidasa. If overnighting in Candidasa, stay at **Puri Bagus Candidasa** (http://puribagus.net), and for an unexpectedly upscale dinner for this laid-back town, go to **Vincent's** (www.vincentsbali.com).

Day 2: East Bali
Water palaces and teaming reefs

From Candidasa, start the day with a visit to **Tenganan** village, one of Bali's few remaining pre-Hindu era (*Bali Aga*) villages. In the not-too-distant past, living behind walls closed to outsiders, the Tengananese have now opened their village to tourists and are happy to share their ancient traditional beliefs and festivals with the world in the hopes of promoting a better understanding of minority groups. You'll see basket weavers here, men writing ancient Balinese script on *lontar* palm leaves and, best of all, women weaving a rare form of double *ikat* (*geringsing*) on which both the warp and the weft threads are dyed with designs before they are woven. Most of the shops are inside people's homes, so you'll get to see those too.

From Tenganan, go to **Amlapura** (once called Karangasem) to visit the king's palace, **Puri Agung Karangasem**, an eccentric blend of Balinese-Hindu, Chinese and European architecture, for a glimpse of the former

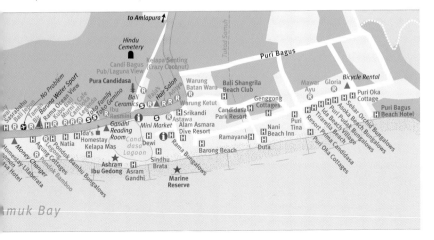

Ujung Water Palace

at **Tulamben**, only 30 km (18 mi.) further up the coast (see page 108). In Amed, don't miss at least one dinner at **Sails Restaurant** up on the cliff. Reservations are advised. Overnight at long-time favorite **Kusuma Jaya Indah cottages** (Tel: 63-363-23488) on Jemeluk beach. Their bungalows are simple but clean, and they have great gardens and an excellent staff.

lives of Balinese royalty. If there's time, make a side trip to the **Ujung Water Palace** (Taman Soekasada Ujung), a complex of three vast pools bordered by fully restored pavilions, which was originally built by a Balinese king in 1901. Rarely crowded, it is a beautiful, serene park in which to stroll around.

The royal bathing pools at **Tirta Gangga** ('Ganges Water'), further north, were constructed in 1948 and are still visited today by Balinese pilgrims, who perform purification rituals here. The gardens are lush and green and the ponds are decorated with ornate water-spouting statues and meandering stepping stones that cross the holy water. If you're ready for lunch, there's a very good restaurant overlooking the pools at **Tirta Ayu Hotel & Restaurant** (http://hoteltirtagangga.com), which is owned by descendants of the royal family.

If overnighting in Candidasa, return to your hotel and spend the rest of the day savoring water activities. Have dinner in another of Candidasa's surprisingly upmarket restaurants, **LaRouge** (http://larougebali.com).

If you've chosen to base yourself in **Amed** for east Bali explorations, Days 1 and 2 above can be visited en route from or to the airport. Snorkeling, diving and relaxing are specialties at beautiful, rural Amed, with popular wreck diving

Day 3: **Pura Besakih & Kintamani**
Drive into an ancient volcano

Get an early start to visit **Pura Besakih** (the 'Mother Temple'), the most important temple complex on the island (see page 115), located high on the slopes of holy Mt Agung, which is responsible for the lava flows and

Underwater landmark

Besakih Temple (Pura Besakih)

gigantic volcanic boulders visible on the east coast road from Tulamben to the north. To see more of the aftermath of Mother Nature's fury, continue on to **Mt Batur** in the Kintamani Highlands, named a UNESCO International Geopark in 2012. Everything about this area is different than the rest of Bali: absent are the family compounds surrounded by ornamental gardens, the people are more aggressive, and it can be bone chillingly cold on windy days, so take a jacket with you.

For a panoramic view into the crater, stop along the road, look down and prepare to be amazed. Strangely beautiful, you can see the remaining walls of the ancient volcano that created this enormous 14 km (8 mi.)-wide hole 20,000 or so years ago, with the waters of Lake Batur sparkling in the sunlight to one side. The view is especially good from **Pura Tegeh Kuripan** (also called Pura Penulisan) at the top of the mountain. A powerful, remote temple complex, its construction began in the 9th century.

A steep flight of stairs rises through the 11 terraces where there are ancient inscriptions and a special temple built by an 11th-century Balinese king for his Chinese wife.

From here, drive down into the arid caldera for a closer look. Drive or trek through the immense caldera floor where house-sized boulders ejected from Mt Batur litter land that is barren and dry except for small patches of irrigated vegetables and reforested sections. Contemplate the power of nature over a lunch of healthy organic foods beside Bali's largest lake at **The Ayu** (www.theayu.com) before returning to Amed or Candidasa for the night.

Time Required Minimum 3 days. **Best Time to Go** During the week to avoid traffic jams and crowds. **Level** Mostly easy, except for steep climbs at some of the temples. **Getting Around** Check to see if your accommodation in either Candidasa or Amed offers a pick-up service at the airport (about 1½ hours to Candidasa and about 2½ hours to Amed via the new east coast highway). If not, take a fixed-price taxi. For day trips, your accommodation can arrange an English-speaking driver.

EXPLORING LOMBOK
Spend a day at the beach and then explore inner Lombok

Locating yourself in Senggigi or further north in Mangsit is ideal for explorations around the island, thanks to their accessibility, gorgeous beaches and many resort choices. If being where the action is appeals, opt for Senggigi, but if a more rural atmosphere is your idea of a dream holiday, choose Mangsit.

Day 1: Senggigi Beach & Central Lombok
A tour of Lombok's temples and handicraft villages

Senggigi Beach is Lombok's main tourist center and it is where the widest range of accommodations, eateries and shops are located. As it expanded to the north, boutique hotels began to spring up in **Mangsit**.

The road to Senggigi Beach

To reach the handicraft villages east of the beaches, you'll pass through **Mataram** and its satellite cities: Ampenan and Cakranegara (locally called Cakra), which flows into Sweta. There are not many tourist attractions here, unless you fancy a stroll through **Ampenan**, a colorful old port town, passing its Arab quarter and rows of shops.

Just outside of the cities is **Lingsar Temple** (Pura Lingsar), built in 1714 and uniquely used by Hindus, Buddhists and adherents of Wetu Telu, an unorthodox Muslim sect. A highly active temple complex, it is not unusual to see pilgrims here, as well as performances of traditional dances by the native Sasak people on ceremonial occasions. Further east is **Narmada Park** (Taman Narmada), whose focal point is a man-made lake in the shape of Anak Segara in the caldera of Mt Rinjani. It is said to have been constructed in 1805 by a Mataram raja after he became too old to climb the holy mountain to deposit offerings in the sacred lake.

Stop for lunch in **Tetebatu**, a beautiful highland area surrounded by plantations literally perched on the southern slopes of active Mt Rinjani. There are no outstanding eateries in this area, but **Wisma Soejono**, now a hotel, is an interesting place for common Indonesian fare because its cafe overlooks fields planted with rice, vanilla, coffee, avocado, tobacco, cloves and other crops. The main building was erected in 1920 in the Dutch 'tropical Indies' style and was the mountain retreat home of a Javanese doctor. If you would like to take a short walk through the plantation, the staff will be happy to show you around.

After lunch, drive to **Pringgasela village**, almost to the east coast, and one of several weaving villages. Lombok is known for its fine handwoven textiles,

some using natural dyes and many still created on backstrap looms. There's an excellent women's co-op here, **Inkra Tanak Gadang Artshop**, and visitors are welcome to wander through a maze of houses to see the various stages of the dyeing and weaving processes and indulge in some shopping.

In addition to weavings, Lombok is internationally acclaimed for its earthenware made from local riverbed clay and fired in pits, using the same methods devised in the 16th century. See the process at New Zealand-assisted **Masbagik village**, and allow time to make a few purchases of items that are exported to other countries and sold at much higher prices.

For overnight options, see page 91. Dine at your hotel.

lifestyle, sans cars and traffic. Your hotel or any of the dive operators can arrange for you to take a day trip to the islands by boat from Sengiggi for snorkeling, diving and sunbathing (see page 108 for dive operators). If you're on Gili Trawangan at lunchtime, eat at **Alam Gili** on the north coast, owned by the daughter of Ubud's Ibu Wayan of the long-time fave Cafe Wayan.

Day 2: The Gili Islands
Spend days lazing on the beach

Just because you're staying on one of the western beaches doesn't mean you can't spend a day in the **Gili Islands** (page 22) to see a totally different type of

Day 3: Craft Villages & Lombok's Kuta Beach
The road to Lombok's southern coast

To see more of Lombok, drive toward the southern beaches, noticing how

Gili Air

Sasak woman separating threads

dry and barren the land is here compared to central and eastern Lombok. Stop at **Banyumulek**, the second of three pottery villages sponsored by a New Zealand aid group (see Masbagik village in Day 1 above). Their assistance has enabled these craftsmen to meet international health and safety standards in their pottery so that their tablewares can be exported. They have also provided training in administrative work to local communities and helped secure markets abroad.

Further south, **Sukarara** is a weaving village where women produce colorful cloths, some of which are *songket*, supplemented with silver or gold threads. Continuing to the south, **Penujak** is the third of Lombok's traditional pottery-making villages, their vases, jugs and tableware featuring animal and gecko figures. Watch how the entire village works together, the women working with wooden paddles to form clay into decorative items and the men tending the firing pits (see page 100 for shopping).

For an excellent lunch overlooking the shimmering sea, stop at **Novotel Lombok Mandalika Resort** on the south coast. Its unique architecture was modeled after traditional Sasak villages, so take a few minutes before you leave to have a look around the resort. You can spend the afternoon on adjoining Kuta or any of the other isolated beaches, or return to Senggigi, stopping in at **Rambitan** and **Sade**, two of Lombok's most traditional Sasak villages. Notice the thatch-roofed **rice storage barns** (*lumbung*) in the two villages, and in Rambitan the 17th-century wooden **Kuno Mosque** (Mesjid Kuno). Visitors are not permitted to enter the mosque, but in both villages local 'guides' will take you around and explain some of the eccentricities of their ancient ways for a small tip.

Time Required Minimum 3 days. **Best Time to Go** If beaches are your first priority, avoid the wet season (November–March) for a more enjoyable holiday, but beware of crowds during the summer months (June–August). **Getting Around** For day trips, hire a car with an English-speaking driver through the travel desk at your hotel.

Gili Meno beach

EXPLORING
KOMODO
Home of unusual wildlife, including the huge 'dragons'

No matter how widely traveled they are, most people will never forget their first encounter with the world's largest lizard, the Komodo dragon. The park contains some of the most beautiful waters in Indonesia, so allow plenty of time for swimming, snorkeling or diving while you're here.

Day 1: Labuan Bajo
Arriving at Komodo airport

There are several ways to prearrange visits to **Komodo National Park**, including dive charters and sea kayaking tours (see page 107), or you can go

the luxury route by sailing from Bali with one of Sea Trek's (www.seatrek-bali.com) two traditional sailing boats (*pinisi*) or the *Adelaar* (www.adelaar-cruises.com), a restored Dutch schooner. If on a tight schedule, though, **Labuan Bajo** on the west coast of Flores is the primary entry point for the park. Get there one day prior to your anticipated Komodo expedition to make arrangements for the boat trip to the park, which your hotel can help you do. An excellent choice of accommodations and meals is **Bajo Komodo Eco Lodge** (www.ecolodges-indonesia.com) because of their dedication to preserving nature and local cultures.

Day 2: Visiting Komodo National Park
'There Be Dragons'

Two of the park's islands, Komodo and Rinca (pronounced 'ren-cha'), are open to visitors, and each offers a unique experience (page 23). Most boats

Labuan Bajo harbor

Komodo dragons

leave Labuan Bajo very early in the morning, and while some offer stops on both islands, others only provide passage to and from Komodo or Rinca, but not both. When making reservations, be sure to choose the outfitter that best suits your expectations.

For a two-island cruise, the driver will select which one will be the first stop based on tides and crowds. It's a two-hour sail to Rinca, which receives fewer visitors, and three hours to Komodo, passing islets and outcroppings interspersed with eddies and swift currents that have protected the lizards' habitat for thousands of years. One of the driest

spots in Indonesia, the park bakes in the heat of the equatorial sun almost year round, and as its mountainous terrain produced nothing of interest to conquerors, it was left virtually untouched except for the few fishermen and pearl divers who dared to go the spot marked on old maps as 'There Be Dragons'.

Only the hardiest flora and fauna species can survive in this environment, but the scrubby monsoon forests teem with birdlife, particularly early in the day. The few mammals on the islands, including crab-eating macaques, wild pigs, buffaloes, horses and a healthy population of Timor deer (*Cervus timorensis*), were probably introduced centuries ago. There are some nasty snakes here, including vipers and cobras, so stay on the paths at all times.

After trekking, most tours include time to swim and snorkel in the crystalline sea at one of several islands that are

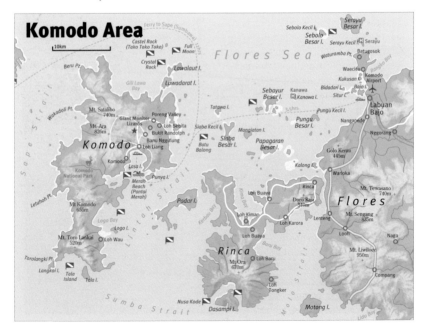

Komodo Area

Snorkeling in pristine waters

part of the park. This is one of the rare occasions that snorkeling is almost as amazing as diving, as in the shallows colorful crinoids, nudibranchs, giant clams and an unbelievable variety of reef fish are abundant in the plankton- and oxygen-rich waters.

If lunch is included on small boats, it's usually a simple Indonesian meal of rice, vegetables and perhaps fish or chicken, returning to Labuan Bajo in the afternoon.

Day 3: Bird-watching, Diving & Snorkeling
Fascinating marine life and wildlife

Take a boat trip designed by Bajo Komodo Eco Lodge (www.ecolodg-esindonesia.com) up nearby Nangenai River for either early morning or late afternoon wildlife spotting to see Wallacea Zone birds of both Australian and Asian origin, monitor lizards, monkeys and hopefully an endangered estuarine crocodile, and spend the rest of the day swimming and snorkeling at **Bidadari Island**. Have lunch and dinner at Bajo Komodo Eco Lodge.

Coral reef life

Time Required Minimum 3 days. **Best Time to Go** Any time except January, February and perhaps March when the seas are very rough in this area, remembering that it will be crowded during summer months (June–August). **Difficulty Level** For the most part easy, with the exception of a steep walk on Rinca Island. As it is very hot here, remember to drink plenty of water to avoid dehydration. Dive only with an experienced dive master due to swift currents and strong undertows. **Getting Around** Bajo Komodo Eco Lodge can arrange all your transportation needs.

EXPLORING
NORTH SUMATRA
A visit to spectacular Lake Toba, the world's largest crater lake

See Medan to Lake Toba, Tuktuk and Parapat maps on folded map.

The tsunamis that affected Sumatra's west coast in the first decade of 2000 caused many people to move the entire island way down on their travel priority lists, which is good news for Lake Toba visitors. Formerly packed to the gills with tourists, you can now enjoy the beauty and serenity of this scenic area without the crowds.

Day 1: From Medan to Berastagi & Parapat
Drive up into the Batak highlands

The gateway to Lake Toba is **Medan**, the crowded, hectic capital of north Sumatra province. If you arrive at breakfast time, stop at **Tip Top Restaurant** (Jl. Jend. A. Yani No. 92), opened in 1934.

Grand mosque in North Sumatra

Within walking distance on the same street, which is lined with European-style buildings, is **Tjong A Fie Mansion**, built by a Chinese merchant in the early 1900s. The Malay-Muslim **Maimun Palace** on Jl. Brigjen Katamso once housed the Sultan of Deli.

The scenic route to Lake Toba from Medan passes through **Berastagi**, a former Dutch hill station about two hours by car from Medan. Its mild climate and natural beauty as a vegetable, flower and fruit farming area, guarded by two active volcanoes, make it a popular rest stop. If it's lunchtime, your driver can recommend where to eat. There's a lookout tower, **Menara Pandangtele**, near Berastagi for awesome views of the northern end of the lake. Nearby is a traditional Karo village, **Lingga**, whose unique architecture, unlike that of their Toba Batak cousins, has a thatched roof. After a quick drive-through, continue on to Parapat.

Tuktuk on Samosir Island has the widest range of accommodations, and to get there your car will be loaded onto a ferry in **Parapat**, and you will be free to sit in an upstairs waiting room or wander around to view the lake during the crossing. Ferries depart Parapat every hour or two, but be aware that they can take one or two hours to disembark arriving passengers and cargo before reloading. Situate yourself in a *warung* (small eatery) near the harbor with a cup of yummy Sumatran coffee and chat with the locals, who love practicing their English, while you wait. Your driver can come to collect you when it's time to board.

Dinner and overnight at **Tabo Cottages** (http://tabocottages.com). It doesn't have a beach, but you can swim in the lake from the shore. Be sure to taste the restaurant's freshly baked breads, special coffee blends and, if you're brave, *kopi*

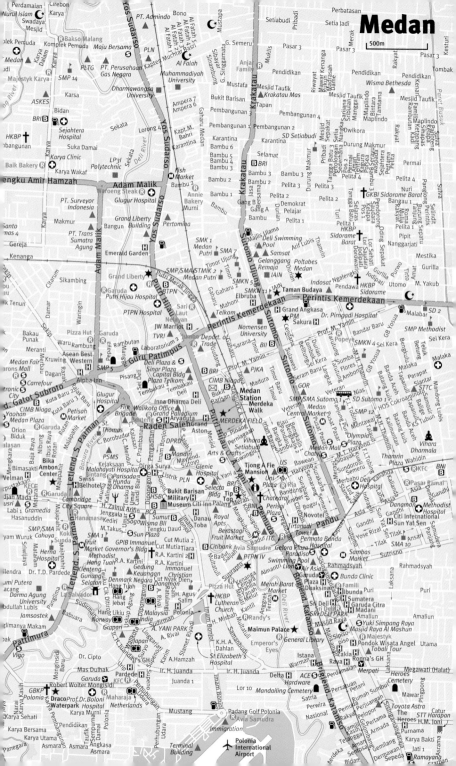

Medan

500m

Tuktuk on Samosir Island, Lake Toba

luwak, made with coffee beans that have been fermented in the digestive tracts of civet cats.

Days 2 & 3: Exploring Samosir Island
The ancient home of Batak culture

Prearrange with your hotel for a car and English-speaking driver or guide to take you around Samosir Island to see some of the Batak antiquities, traditional houses and outstanding scenery (page 20). Your guide will choose an appropriate lunch spot when it's time to eat. For dinner, check to see if nearby **Samosir Cottages** has a Batak band singing while you're there. Their sheer enthusiasm will entice you to sing along, even if you don't know the words.

Lake Toba's laid-back atmosphere is perhaps its second biggest attraction after its setting, so plan at least one day to do nothing more than just 'be' without any pressing schedules to meet. If you need more action than simply reading a good book while gazing out over the lake, Tabo Cottages rents bicycles or you can

stroll on your own to traditional villages and farms that are close by. Tuktuk's main street is lined with kiosks selling soft drinks and souvenirs that beg to be perused. Have lunch at **Juwita Cafe**. Heddy, the owner and an excellent chef, also gives cooking classes.

Lake Toba Batak house

Time Required Minimum 3 days. **Best Time to Go** Dry season (April–October). **Getting Around** Tabo Cottages can arrange all your transportation needs.

See Minang Highlands map on folded map.

The capital of West Sumatra is the coastal city of Padang, the starting point for an exploration of the surrounding Minang Highlands. The hardy Minang people are known throughout Indonesia for their spicy hot cuisine, canny business sense and unique matriarchal traditions. The landscape is fertile valleys that have been cultivated for hundreds of years, surrounded by beautiful volcanoes and mountain ranges, making it one of Sumatra's most memorable areas.

Days 1 & 2: Bukit Tinggi & Lake Maninjau
Visiting the Minang homeland

Journeys into the cool climes of the Minang Highlands begin in **Padang** on Sumatra's west coast. Padang's claim to fame is its spicy food, the most ubiquitous of which is *rendang sapi*, chunks of beef simmered in a coconut curry that will set your mouth on fire. Try it at **Pagi Sore** (Jl. Pondok 143) in Padang. To get to Bukit Tinggi from the airport (about two hours over good roads), hop in a fixed-price taxi at the taxi counter.

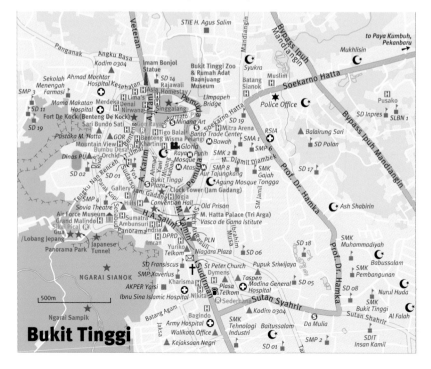

Clock Tower (Jam Gadang)

Upon arrival in **Bukit Tinggi** (page 21), the first order of business is to get situated in your hotel and get acquainted with the layout of the town before venturing out into the countryside. Overnight and dinner at the **Grand Rocky Hotel Bukit Tinggi** (www.rockyhotelsgroup.com), within walking distance of the town square.

The refreshing climate and friendly folks in Bukit Tinggi are a welcome relief after traveling. Stroll around the town to see the sites, then hire a car with an English-speaking driver and head west out into the countryside for some awe-inspiring scenery. **Lake Maninjau** (Danau Maninjau) is an ancient crater lake whose slopes are studded with picturesque villages and dense forests that are ideal for walking or cycling, or relaxing in a coffee shop by the lake. Pass through Matur, skirting the foot of Bukit Kapanasan before reaching the crater's rim at **Embun Pagi** for panoramic views of the lake. A higher lookout point at **Puncak Lawang** is north of here, and downhill near **Bayua** are several villages with **traditional houses** (*rumah gadang*) still in use. Your driver can recommend a nice place near the lake for a leisurely lunch.

As you pass through highland villages, notice how few men there are. This is due to an ancient Minangkabau matrilineal custom that encourages boys and men to go out in the world and seek their fortunes while the women manage the houses and farmlands. Loyal sons send the lion's share of their earnings back home to their mothers to help her maintain family assets.

Have dinner tonight at **Bedudal Cafe** (Jalan A. Yani No. 95), which serves excellent Indonesian food as well as sandwiches, pizza and steaks. Tourist information is available here and English is spoken.

Sianok Canyon

Day 3: Minang Weaving & Traditional Architecture
Glimpses of Sumatran tribal culture

Continue your explorations of the highlands by traveling south of Bukit Tinggi. The royal Minang court was located in this area from the 14th to 19th centuries, and several *rumah gadang* (literally 'big house') remain

Traditional Minang house

in use in the region. Elegant elongated rectangular structures, their roofs are gabled and rise to peaks at either end to represent buffalo horns based on ancient Minang folklore. The houses are divided into a number of apartments, each occupied by women related to the matriarch of the household. The carvings on the sides of the houses are each symbolic, reminding their inhabitants of the proper way to behave in society.

Before exploring a few *rumah gadang* villages, stop first in **Pandai Sikek**, where handwoven cloths embroidered with metallic threads, called *songket*, are made by many of the women in a thriving cottage industry. Highly sought after by elite Jakarta ladies, the more elaborate cloths can run from thousands to millions of rupiah. If there's time, stop at the **Center for Documentation and Information on Minangkabau Culture** (PDIKM), a traditional Minang house-cum-museum, in Padang Panjang.

East of Padang Panjang is **Batipuh**, where there's a large men's house

(*surau*) constructed in the aristocratic Koto Piliang style. Just after Batipuh, turn off to the left (northeast) and up the steep slopes of Mt Marapi to **Pariangan**, set in a picturesque valley with stairways leading to traditional houses, large ponds and a royal tomb. The *surau* here is one of the last of its kind still in use. Legend has it that this village was the original settlement of the Minangkabau ancestors who descended from Mt Marapi's peak. On the way back, stop in at **Tabek** village to see several examples of old Minang architecture. The council hall (Balairung Sari) is believed to be the oldest building in west Sumatra, and the scenery here is nothing short of spectacular. Let your driver suggest a place to stop for lunch before heading back to Bukit Tinggi. Dinner at your hotel.

Time Required Minimum 3 days. **Best Time to Go** Dry season (April–October). **Difficulty Level** For the most part easy, with the exception of a steep walk at Pariangan. **Getting Around** Grand Rocky Hotel Bukit Tinggi can arrange all your transportation needs.

*See Tana Toraja map and Rantepao
insert on folded map.*

Touring in Tana Toraja is akin to visiting the fabled Shangri-La. Isolated since the beginning of time by distant mountains and rugged granite outcrops, its valleys are filled with fertile rain-fed rice terraces dotted with curved-roof traditional houses. Although most Torajan are Christians, their elaborate funerary rites, including animal sacrifices, have gained international notice.

Day 1: Arrival in Makassar
The journey to Toraja via Makassar

South Sulawesi's provincial capital, **Makassar**, whose airport, oddly enough, still goes by the old name Ujung Pandang, is the first step toward reaching Tana Toraja. Flights from Kuala Lumpur, Singapore and other Indonesian cities arrive here daily. Makassar's most notable heritage site is **Fort Rotterdam**, built in 1545, and now the LaGaligo Museum. Perched on the waterfront, alongside is **Losari Beach Esplanade** featuring hotels, eateries and entertainment.

In the very recent past, the only way to get from Makassar to **Rantepao**, the gateway to Tana Toraja, was a grueling seven-hour drive over winding mountain roads at breakneck speeds by car or bus. Thankfully, there are now two flights a week (Tuesdays and Fridays) with SMAC (Sabang Merauke Air Charter) that cater to tourists. Although the absence of daily flights requires careful planning, Tana Toraja is worth the effort. Take a sweater; it's chilly here in the mornings and after sunset.

Upon arrival at your hotel, the first order of business is to enquire if there are any funeral ceremonies being held in the vicinity. Although June–July is the regular 'season', you might get lucky even if you are there during other months. Second, find out which day the weekly traditional market is held in Makale so you can arrange your schedule to attend funeral rituals and be in Makale on those days. You might need to rearrange the itineraries below, which your guide can help you do, in order to accommodate these events. Overnight and dinner at **Toraja Heritage Hotel** (www.torajaheritage.com).

Day 2: Exploring Sites South of Rantepao
Traditional Torajan villages

Today drive south of Rantepao to visit several villages that have maintained their traditional houses and unique gravesites. **Ke'te Kesu**, just south of Rantepao, is the oldest one, and is idyllically situated in a virtual sea of rice fields. All tourists stop here, so don't be surprised if it's crowded; rather, pause on the hill for a moment to focus on the beauty of this place before going down to enter the village. The houses, called *tongkonan*, are lined up in a row facing

WEST SULAWESI

South Sulawesi

SOUTH SULAWESI

Makassar Strait

Bone Bay

Mandar Bay

TANA TORAJA

Makassar (Ujung Pandang)

20km

Tapalang
Mt. Gandadiwata 3074m
2117m
Taba
Batusitanduk
Lamasi
Amassangan
Mambi
2176m
2335m
Sangkaropi
Walenrang
Rantepang
Tokaili
Buttu Panda 1336m
Mamasa
Rindingallo
Rantepao
Tana Toraja Culture
Rantepang
Batu Putih
Labombo Beach
Lamikomiko Estuary
to Teluk Ussu
Malunda
alutambung
Tandialo
Paurrungan
Bittuang
Batan
Sipate
Ampadang
Palopo
Beringinjaya
Padangkalua
1517m
Balambang
Sipatte
Rea
Typical Torajan Villages
Sanggala
Padangsappa
Bua
to Kolaka
Buttu Tamanipi 1181m
Buttu Parinding 2619m
Karoan
Tangratte
Makale
Getengan
Buntu Tampatoraja 912m
Ponrang
Patedong
Olong Pt.
Sumarorong
Mangngi
+2020m
Buakayu
Beuma
Ponrang Estuary
Bauma
Banejambong Pt.
Buttu Tamedingin 1296m
Kalitarung
Buttu Waylimbong 1743m
Kondodewata
Lumbaja
Belajen
Patongan
Buntu Rantemario 3478m
Padangsappa
Babana
Bajo
Belopa
Cilallang
Pandengpareng
Andau
Capego
Rampusa
Baraka
+2674m
Tibusan
Lempokasi
Cimpu
Bumbung
Wonomulyo
Polewali
Panassang
Cakke
Dantemalua
Botto Tallu 3086m
Larompong
Paletoan
Campalagian
Karawa
Dadeko
Enrekang
Botto Lebu +1322m
Majene
Tinambung
Kayuanging
Kassa
Tambolang
Pampieo Mampie Reserve
Panampeang Estuary
Buttu Pasapaa 1534m
to Susua
Lampa
Teppo
Malimpung
Maiwa
Siwa
Sadang Estuary
Cempapasar
Baranti
Larumpu
Poselloreng
Lokoloko Point
to Kolaka
Pinrang
Rappang
Tanrutedong
Anabanua
Marasanga Island
Langnga
Lapalopo
Uluale
Sidenreng
Tellang Island
Harapankarya
Amparita
Paria
Pare Pare
Tancung
Jalang
Ujunglero
Lappakaka
Batubatu
Lake Sidenreng
Lake Tempe
Sengkang
Lakamporo
Palanro
Palicu
Silk Weaving
Maroanging
Wawagalung
Kotabaru
Tawaru
Mangkoso
Donridoni
Pampanua
Uloe
Pallime
Watansoppeng
Cabbenge
Mampu Caves
Tokaseng
to Kolaka
Galung
Coppo Mabolae 1253m
Cangadi
Macope
Kampung Tenga
Nampo
Takalala
Taccipi
Watampone
Pekkae
Kessi
Bajoe
Tamarupa Barat
Ralla
Ponreng
Apala
Ujung Patitiro
Segeri
Jembulu
Lalebata
Matango
Buludua
Pattiro Bajo
Bontobonto
Bulu Marukuruku 1335m
Lawelu
Benrongeng
802m
Kadai
Binangatoa
Labakkang
1687m
Tanabatue
Camming
Salongketo Point
Lejang
Tumampua
Toceppa
Bulubulu
Pangkajene
Padangtangalu
Kalibong
Palattae
Balange
Talawe
Camba
Sembilan Islands
Barrang Caddi Island
Kasuarang
Bantimurung
Kahu
Bojo
Batanglempe I.
Maros
Bantimurung Reserve
Waterfall, Caves
Bulu Bualo 1504m
Bulupodo
Sinjai
Kambuno I.
Burungloe I.
Mandai
Bikeru
Samataring
Batusantung
Trans Studio Theme Park
Losari Beach
Biringkanaya
Bontobotoa
Manrojai
Lappadata
Fort Rotterdam & Museum
Patuku
Hill Resort
Sungguminasa
Parang
Malino
Amesangeng
Kassi
Bontolebang
Limbung
Ballalompoa Museum
Mt. Lompobattang 2871m
Tanete
Tanuntung
Galesong
Sapaya
Lompobattang Reserve
Pattallasang
+618m
Hilahila
Satanga Island
Takalar
Pangngamarang
Malakaji
Gantarangkeke
Tanahberu
Bauluang Island
Cilalang
Mangadu
Pukangang
Pullaweng
Bulukumba
Tanekeke Island
Allu
Panaikang
Bantaeng
Bissapu Waterfall
Ponre
Bira
Makareso Beach
Ujung Pepe
Teneta
Togotogo
Bontowa
Ujungkatingting
Ujung Bira
Laikang Bay
Jeneponto
Bontosunggu
Liukanglu Island
Ujung Mangasa
Malosoro Bay
to Badas, Baubau, Bonerate, Labuanbajo, Maumere

Traditional Torajan houses

almost identically carved rice barns. More than simply a place to dwell, one's *tongkonan* is an important link to familial ties. Torajans may not know all the names of distant relatives, but they always remember which house their parents and grandparents were born in.

Behind the village are the ancestral burial cliffs without their effigies (*tau-tau*), which have been removed for safe-keeping. To one side are 'hanging graves' in the cliffside, with bones and skulls scattered below that have spilled out of decayed wooden coffins.

Lemo village is further south and has one of the most impressive cliff graves in the region, with dozens of effigies staring unseeingly from high above. The *tau-tau* are believed to be the receptacle of the ghost of the deceased. In this village, only wealthy high-caste individuals are allowed to be buried in the cliff, whose tombs are chipped out of the granite by hand. Others are placed in a cemetery nearby, some with elaborate headstones.

If it's market day, continue on to **Makale**, where their colorful *pasar* (traditional market) presents more photo ops than can be imagined. Fruits and vegetables, chickens and fish, beaded handicrafts and everything else a family needs, including plastic pails and toothbrushes, can be purchased here. Your guide will recommend a lunch stop, depending on which route you take.

If interested in seeing some of the countryside on foot, there is an easy trek from Karuaya to Radan Batu passing megalithic stones and both old and new *tongkonan*. Dinner at your hotel.

Day 3: **A Scenic Drive**
Rice fields and cliffside graves

Spend a little time in Rantepao and see **handwoven *ikat* textiles** being created at Todi Weaving Shop (Jalan Pembangunan No. 19, http://www.todi.co.id). This is a women's co-op designed to bring the cloths of isolated village weavers to buyers skipping the middleman merchant, who often pays little for them and reaps large profits for himself. In *ikat* making, bundles of threads are tied, dyed and dried many times to create motifs before placing them on the loom, and you can see how this intricate process is done, in addition to the weaving itself. The shop also sells t-shirts, handicrafts and other souvenirs. If you want to buy some Torajan coffee to take home, ask your guide to stop at one of several local shops that will allow you to choose the quality of beans that you prefer.

Rice fields

After shopping, drive north of Rantepao to **Deri** along a road that passes beautiful green rice fields littered with graves carved out of gigantic boulders scattered throughout the valley. Have a relaxing lunch at **Mentirotiku Resto** at **Batu Tumonga**, which is perched atop a cliff overlooking a scenic valley. After lunch, go for a short walk down the paved main road to spot gorgeous

butterflies, huge moths and interesting insects, such as rhinoceros beetles. Dinner at your hotel.

Time Required Minimum 3 days. **Best Time to Go** Dry season (April–October). Note that Makassar is in the same time zone as Bali, thus one hour ahead of Jakarta time. **Getting Around** A car and driver with an English-speaking guide is recommended for the duration of your stay in Tana Toraja. Pre-booking with Wira Tours & Travel in Makassar (www.sulawesi-celebes.com) can arrange pick-up at the Rantepao Airport and transfer to your hotel, as well as hotel reservations and your guide.

Torajan cliffside effigies

EXPLORING NORTH SULAWESI
A Christian enclave and some of Indonesia's best diving

See Manado Area map on folded map.

Although diving in Bunaken National Park is North Sulawesi's most prominent claim to fame, within easy day trips from the provincial capital of Manado are some of the island's unique animal species which can be seen on forest walks. North Sulawesi is also home to the fun-loving, primarily Christian Minahasa people known for their penchant for spicy exotic foods.

Day 1: Manado & the Minahasa Highlands
The road to scenic Lake Tondano

The bustling capital of north Sulawesi province, **Manado**, is the entry point for Bunaken Marine National Park. Aside from expansive views of the bay, there isn't much to see in the city. Apart from a gigantic hilltop statue of Jesus Christ welcoming visitors and bestowing blessings on Manado City, the only other places of interest are the 335-year-old **Ban Hin Kiong Temple** in the Chinatown area and the first Protestant church built by the Dutch, **Gereja Centrum**.

Just outside of Manado, at **Tinoor** village, stop briefly for views of the city from 550 m (1,805 ft) above sea level,

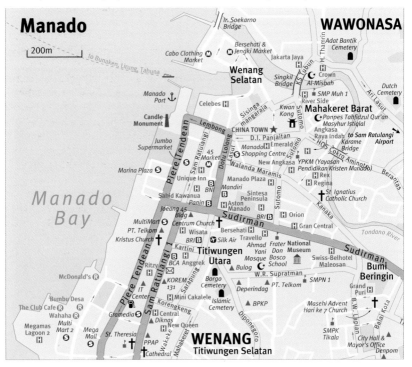

Diving on a coral sea wall off Bunaken Island

then drive south towards **Tomohon**, the 'City of Flowers', in the beautiful **Minahasa Highlands**. Situated in the saddle between two active volcanoes, Mts Mahawu and Lokon, the climate here is delightfully temperate, and a wide range of fruit and flower plantations pepper the hills. On the way, at **Bukit Doa** (Prayer Hill), there are several Christian churches and a Buddhist temple, Pagoda Ekayana, surrounded by picturesque countryside. Just before Tomohan is **Rurukan**, bordered by vegetable plantations as far as the eye can see, where there is an authentic traditional house. Nearby is **Woloan**, a small village where knock-down Minahasa-style houses are built for export.

Around **Lake Tondano** are ever-changing vistas of nearby mountains, rice fields and the lake itself. Have lunch at one of the fish restaurants on the lake recommended by your guide. Starting back toward Manado, see the pottery-making process at **Pulutan** village and local weaving workshops. The final stop is for afternoon tea or coffee at the sulfurous **Lake Linow**, which constantly changes color. Dinner at **Raja Sate BBQ & Asian Restaurant** (Jl. Piere Tendean No. 39, near Mega Mall). Stay overnight

at **Sintesa Peninsula Hotel** (http://manado.sintesapeninsulahotel.com).

Days 2 & 3: Diving & Wildlife Explorations
Sulawesi's extraordinary wildlife

The spectacular sea gardens located one hour offshore of Manado in **Bunaken National Park** (page 25) contain an unbelievable abundance of marine life, making it one of Indonesia's most impressive diving spots. The submarine trench reaching to depths of 1,200 m (4,000 ft) that separates the park's islands from the mainland also shield them from the pollution and silt generated in nearby coastal villages, making visibility superb.

The entire tip of the peninsula to the north and east is covered in lush tropical forest, and living in these jungles are some of the world's oddest creatures. Separated from other land masses for millennia, Sulawesi's fauna species have evolved and new ones have come into being that aren't found anyplace else on earth. Described in *The Malay Archipelago* by Sir Alfred Russel Wallace, who traveled through this area in the 19th century, there are at least

Babirusa

five endemic species of macaques, the world's smallest buffalo (*anoa*), a strange pig-deer (*babirusa*), whose upper canine teeth grow upward piercing the skin of its nose, and countless birds, including the odd ground-dwelling maleo that buries its large eggs in sand-covered pits. Many of these unusual creatures are protected in **Tangkoko-Batuangus-Dua Saudara Nature Reserve**, just over two hours by car east of Manado. Take an easy rainforest walk in search of them, as well as tiny tarsiers, the marsupial cuscus, elegant hornbills and other Wallacea birds.

When you've had your fill, drive a bit further to have a vegetarian lunch with the local staff and volunteers from throughout the world at **Tasikoki Wildlife Rescue & Education Center** (www.tasikoki.org). Over 200 animals of more than 40 species that have been rescued, largely from the illegal wildlife trade, are housed here and are nursed back to health, then rehabilitated to be returned to the wild. Visit the education center, designed to help local people find sustainable alternatives to poaching, the Primate, Reptile and Avian Centers and the Herbivore Sanctuary. The property also has an eco-lodge and volunteer opportunities. Dinner at **Rumah Makan Green Garden** (Jl. Sam Ratulangi) in Manado.

Time Required Minimum 2 days. **Best Time to Go** Dry season (April–October). **Getting Around** To see the most in a short time, book a car and driver, English-speaking guide and your hotel through Safari Tours & Travel in Manado (www.manadosafaris.com).

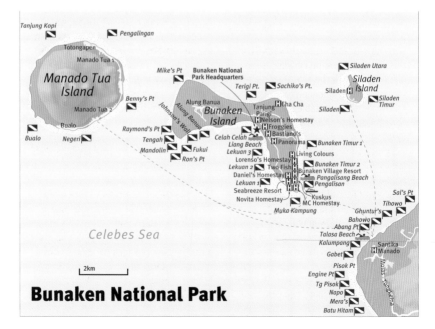

Tanjung Kopi
Pengalingan
Totongapen
Manado Tua 1
Mike's Pt   Bunaken National Park Headquarters   Siladen Utara
Manado Tua Island   Terigi Pt.   Sachiko's Pt.   *Siladen Island*
Benny's Pt   Alung Banua   Siladen   Siladen Timur
Manado Tua 2   Johnson's Wall   **Bunaken Island**   Tanjung Parigi   Cha Cha   Siladen
Bualo   Raymond's Pt   Nelson's Homestay
Bualo   Negeri   Tengah   Celah Celah   Bastiano's   Froggies
Mandolin   Fukui   Liang Beach   Panorama   Bunaken Timur 1
Ron's Pt   Lekuan 3   Living Colours
Lorenso's Homestay   Bunaken Timur 2
Lekuan 2   Two Fish   Bunaken Village Resort
Daniel's Homestay   Pangalisang Beach
Lekuan 1   Pengalisan
Seabreeze Resort   Sal's Pt
Novita Homestay   MC Homestay   Kuskus   Tihowo
Muka Kampung   Ghuntur's
Bahowo
Abang Pt
Celebes Sea   Talasa Beach
Kalumpang   Santika
Gabet   Manado
Pisok Pt
2km   Engine Pt
Tg Pisok
Napo
Mera's
Batu Hitam

Bunaken National Park

EXPLORING
PAPUA
An unforgettable journey
to the remote Baliem Valley

Visiting the Baliem Valley isn't for everyone. Its remoteness, lack of five-star amenities, the time it takes to travel to and from Papua, and the necessity of walking from village to village make it unattractive to many. But for the adventurer who savors unique experiences, this is one you'll never forget.

Day 1: Jayapura
The gateway to Indonesian Papua

To sojourn in Papua, visitors must obtain a travel permit (*surat jalan*) in **Jayapura** before beginning their journey. For the best use of your time, rather than sitting in a government office waiting for the required paperwork, it is recommended to book your tour through a reputable local agency, allowing them to handle the bureaucracy while you begin your holiday.

The *surat jalan* can be obtained up to one month prior to arrival, so if you have already sent your documentation to the local agent he will meet you in Sentani, where the airport is located, with *surat jalan* in hand, and you will take the connecting flight to Wamena, the gateway to the Baliem Valley. If you have not pre-arranged your *surat jalan*, he will meet you at the airport and ask you for a photocopy of your passport, two passport-sized photos, and your embarkation card. (Confirm with the agency when you book your reservations that this is all they need, as requirements change frequently.) His representative will then drive to nearby Jayapura to obtain the permit for you while you see a few sites.

Museum Loka Budaya at Cendrawashih University in Abepura, between Jayapura and Sentani, and nearby **Museum Negeri** display artifacts from throughout Papua and collections from the Dutch era and are a good introduction to some of the cultures you will encounter during your visit. Kiosks at both places sell carvings and craft items. World War II buffs may choose to skip the museums and instead drive up to Mt Ifar (6 km/3.7 mi.) to see the **General McArthur Monument**, where it is said he sat overlooking the massive expanse of Lake Sentani below while developing his strategy for the Pacific invasion.

Lunch will be on the beautiful **Lake Sentani**, which your agent will arrange for you. Ask if the dates for the annual Lake Sentani Festival, which varies from June to August, coincide with your visit, as it offers a fun-filled day of performances, handicrafts and games. Fly to Wamena. Overnight at **Hotel Baliem Pilamo** (Jalan Trikora). Dinner at hotel.

Day 2: Wamena to Jiwika
Encounter with a mummy

The flight from Jayapura to Wamena takes 45 minutes in a small commuter sized plane and enters the vast **Baliem Valley** (page 24) by passing over massive peaks that protected it from outside visitors until 1938. **Wamena**, lying at the center of the valley, was established only 30 years later as an

Mummified Dani warrior, Jiwika village

Several villages in this valley possess the desiccated skeletal remains of former heroes, which are kept in the men's houses as a conduit to the supernatural world to obtain good health, bountiful harvests, plenty of wives and pigs, and victory in battle. Keep your camera ready at all times and the batteries charged to the max. For an extra fee, your guide may be able to prearrange a traditional pig feast in one of the nearby villages for you (request this when you arrive in Wamena), an event you won't want to miss.

Lunch will be at your guide's discretion. Have dinner at **Mentari Restoran** (Jl. Yos Sudarso No. 47) in Wamena. Try the grilled crayfish (*udang sungai*), if they have any during your visit.

administrative center for the region. It consists of just a few streets with a traditional market (see Day 4 below), a row of simple accommodations, and a few cafes and souvenir shops catering to tourists. If you arrive on a Sunday, however, it's interesting to see tribal Christians arriving from villages near and far headed for church wearing various forms of their Sunday best dress, ranging from traditional to modern clothing. In August each year, the town comes alive for the Baliem Valley Cultural Festival.

Begin your exploration of this anthropological wonder by driving to **Jiwika** to trek about 300 m (1,020 ft) up the mountain to a **brine pool** where Danis and other tribes make salt exactly as their forebears have done for centuries. Afterward, join them in **Akima** village to see the **mummy** of an ancient warrior.

Day 3: Hike to Kurima
Stunning vistas and Dani villages

Get a close, personal look at the valley floor and the people who live there by first driving to **Sogokmo** village, where the road ends, and then an easy walk about 3 km (1.9 mi.) to **Kurima**. Walking alongside the raging Baliem River, you'll see stunning valley vistas, sweet potato and sugar cane fields and

Traditional Dani village

Baliem Valley

5km

Roggee River
Tagime
Bolokme
Yugwa
Algonik
Jalenga
Manda
Meagaima
Pyramid
Kimbim
Paruba
Rimbim River
Wikuda Caves
Uwosilimo (Wosi)
Wo'ogi
Mummy
Waga-waga
Asologais
Mustafak
BALIEM VALLEY
Elagaima
Ibele Bawah
Ibele Atas
Mulibaga
Isonak
Pondok Yapokuema
Thaila
Yabogaima
Napua
Walaek
The Valley of The Tree Fern's
Elarek
Apikmok
Pabilolo
Kanopa
Somalek Caves
Trikora Peaks (4467 m)

to Landikma
Wolo
Ilugua
Goundal
Yogolok Caves
Warak River
Yomosimo
Wedanku
Ikipalekma
Mosiem
Iluerainma (Iluwe)
Kotilala Caves
Sumpaima
Mummy
Brine Pool
Jiwika
Wenabubuga
Kurulu
Mulima
Warabaga
Wuperainma
Tanahmerah
Dukum (Dugum)
Elabukara
Siobara
Tulem
Aikima
Mummy
Pike
White Sand
Pabuma
Hom-hom
Anlagak
Wamena
Suspension Bridge
Honelama
Sinatma
Wesaput
Pugima
Ilare
Megapura
Walisi
Hepoba
Hetegima
Sogokmo
Salt Spring
Yetni
Kurima
Stunning Views
Tangma
Wamerek

Maki, Tiom, river, Mulia
Balim River
Halim River
Ibele River
Uwen River
Handi River
Kulagema River
Baliem River
Wamena River
Uwe River

Wamena

Hotel Wamena
Petikele Market
to Pasar Jibama, Terminal Jibama, Aikima, Baliem Valley Resort
Patimura
Baliem Pilamo
Blambangan
Mas Budi
Agro Segar
Putri Dani
Irian
Irian
Pelangi
Tawes
Srikandi
Merpati
Irian
Bank Mandiri
Remuja
Wamena Plaza
Pramuka
Departemen Kesehatan
Bhayangkara
Ambon
Nayak
Timor
BRI
MAF
Airport Terminal
Iran
Irian
Bhayangkara
to Honelama
Yos Sudarso
Yos Sudarso
DPRD
to Wesaput
Susi Air
to Sinatma
Bupati's Office
Diponegoro
to Sinatma
STADION PENDIDIKAN
Sumba
Syahrial
Makmur
Bhayangkara
Sudirman
Sudirman
M.H. Thamrin
SD Percobaan
Ahmad Yani
Gatot Subroto
Trikora
Pramuka
Gatot Subroto
M.H. Thamrin
Ahmad Yani
Panjaitan
Trikora
Jawa
Gatot Subroto
JB Wenas
Wouma Market
to Sugokmo
RSUD
500m

Dani villages. Though Christian missionaries have convinced many villagers that clothing is a good idea, and you'll see shorts and t-shirts in Wamena, in the countryside you're more likely to encounter traditional attire: naked men sporting carefully cultivated gourds on their penises and bare-breasted women in grass skirts carrying heavy loads of garden vegetables, a small prized pig or even a baby in woven bags suspended from the tops of their heads. Occasionally, you'll pass women covered in mud in mourning for a lost relative and, more rarely, one who practices the age-old tradition of having a finger joint removed as a sacrifice to placate the ghosts of loved ones.

Dani huts are round, thatched affairs built on a framework of saplings bound with vines, and villages are dominated by a men's hut, with the women and children sleeping separately in other buildings. There's usually an isolated shed where meals are cooked and another where pigs are kept. In the fields, men do the digging and maintain the irrigation system, and women plant and harvest, with all work shared communally. A man's wealth is gauged by how many wives and pigs he possesses.

Before setting out, discuss with your guide your preference as to how much walking you want to do. You can return to Wamena by car from Kurima if you choose, or hardier trekkers can cross a suspension bridge on foot and return to Wamena by walking on the opposite side of the river. Lunch will be arranged by your guide. Dinner at the hotel.

Day 4: Wamena
Explore village folk and handicrafts

Before catching your flight back to Jayapura, visit the Wamena **traditional market** and be sure to bring your camera. Village folk come from miles around to sell not only their vegetables and pigs but also handicrafts, such as the woven *noken* bags that the women wear suspended from their heads and *koteka* (penis gourds) donned by men, both of which make memorable souvenirs of your visit. Note that, traditionally, *noken* bags are made from the fibers of a local plant, but nowadays some are made from colorful yarns bought at the market.

If there is enough time, drive to Wesaput, where there is a **suspension bridge**, for one last photo shoot before departing.

Time Required Minimum 4 days. **Best Time to Go** Dry season (April–October). The Baliem Cultural Festival is held every August prior to Independence Day, August 17, and is a sight to behold, with local dances, feasts and mock war games. **Getting Around** Booking your trip through an experienced local agent will save you a lot of hassles (see Day 1, above). Jefalgi Tours Papua (http://jefalgitours.com) is highly recommended for its sensitivity to the local people as well as to travelers.

Dani man

This chapter is designed to help you find the best of the best that Indonesia offers its guests. A good place to begin planning your trip is locating its hippest hotels and resorts, followed by what and where to eat. From there, move on to shop-'til-you-drop opportunities and the hottest nightlife to be found. Keep reading, because next is where to go for an hour—or a day—to rejuvenate, followed by outdoor activities—sports, hikes and eco-trips—and adventures guaranteed to make kids smile. Last but not least, for the grown-ups (and some kids) is where some of the country's most interesting antiquities are found.

Hippest Hotels & Resorts

Jakarta
Central Java
East Java
South Bali
Central Bali
West Bali
North Bali
Lombok

Best Foods & Restaurants

Java
Bali
Lombok
Sumatra
Sulawesi

Best Shopping

Jakarta
Bandung
Yogyakarta
Bali
Lombok

Hippest Nightlife

Jakarta
Bali

Best Spas & Health Retreats

Java
Central Bali
North Bali

Best Outdoor Activities

Cycling
Diving & Snorkeling
Golf
Kayaking
Rafting
Hikes & Eco-Trips

Best Kid-Friendly Activities

Jakarta & West Java
Central Java
Bali

Best Temples & Museums

Jakarta
Central Java
East Java
Bali

INDONESIA'S HIPPEST HOTELS & RESORTS

JAKARTA

The Dharmawangsa Jakarta
Its understated elegance combined with a relaxing ambience are only two of the charms of The Dharmawangsa Jakarta. Situated in a residential area away from the city center's hubbub, yet near enough to the Central Business District to be convenient, it provides five-star luxury without pomposity. Excellent restaurants, a fabulous bar and a lounge cozy enough to hold intimate conversations in are pluses, and don't forget to leave enough time for one of the divine spa treatments in its Wellness Center.
Jl. Brawijaya Raya No. 26, Kebayoran Baru, Jakarta, Tel: (62-21) 725-8181, www.the-dharmawangsa.com

Harris Suites fX Sudirman
A young, hip and trendy option in the heart of the Central Business District for those who need to be in the region for work but want to opt out of the city traffic gridlock and five-star prices.
Connected to the fX Lifestyle X'nter Mall, Harris Suites fX Sudirman is also within walking distance of most of the downtown tourist attractions and more shopping and entertainment malls, great eateries and bars. Fabulous views from the top floor suites.
Jl. Jend. Sudirman, Pintu Satu Senayan, Jakarta, Tel: (62-21) 2555-4333, http://fx-jakarta.harrishotels.com

Hotel Indonesia Kempinski
The rather unexciting exterior of Hotel Indonesia Kempinski is not a renovation oversight; rather, it's a nod to its historic past as Jakarta's first downtown hotel. In the heart of the Central Business District, at its front is the Welcome Statue and at the rear one of Southeast Asia's largest shopping complexes. Behind the camouflaging facade are glass and chrome, glitter, glamor and luxury, a rooftop spa and all the five-star attributes, coupled with excellent service. It even has a Little VIP program to entertain kids while you work or shop.
Jl. MH Thamrin 1, Jakarta, Tel: (62-21) 2358-3800, www.kempinski.com

CENTRAL JAVA

d'Omah Hotel Yogyakarta
If staying in a village in a traditional Javanese teakwood house refurbished with modern conveniences appeals,

d'Omah Hotel Yogyakarta

d'Omah Hotel Yogyakarta bids you a warm welcome. Only 20 minutes from downtown Jogja, each of the four residences has its own swimming pool and attached living space and is decorated with antiques and Indonesian contemporary art. Fitness and wellness center, Jacuzzi and sauna and yoga space are surrounded by gorgeous gardens flanked by rice fields. Ahhhhh…

Jl. Parangtritis Km 8.5, Tembi village, Timbulharjo, Sewon, Bantul, Yogyakarta, Tel: (62-274) 368-050, http://yogyakartaaccommodation.com

Dusun Jogja Village Inn

While its eco-friendly award deserves kudos, the other main charm of Dusun Jogja Village Inn is that of an oasis away from the bustling world. Located 10 minutes from busy Jalan Malioboro in a vibrant neighborhood surrounded by art galleries and cafes, once inside calmness radiates. In a compact space, its saltwater swimming pool is in the center of gorgeous gardens with secluded conversation nooks surrounded by rooms furnished in earth tones. It's a marvelous escape after a day of touring.

Jl. Menukan 5, Karangkajen, Yogyakarta, Tel: (62-274) 373-31, www.jvidusun.co.id

MesaStila Wellness Retreat

The quiet serenity of a working coffee plantation surrounded by majestic volcanoes three hours north of Jogja is the ideal setting for the environmental award-winning MesaStila Wellness Retreat. Its villas are lovingly restored traditional Javanese houses with modern amenities, and the Club House was formerly the residence of a Dutch planter. Destress and Indulgence, Fitness and Weight Management, Recharge and Cleansing are a few of its packages, complementing the only Hamman spa in Southeast Asia.

Desa Losari, Grabag, Magelang, Tel: (62-298) 596-333, www.mesahotelsandresorts.com

Amanjiwo Resort

Opulent and fabulous, award-winning Amanjiwo Resort is one hour north of Jogja overlooking Borobudur, the world's largest Buddhist monument. If you are able to tear yourself away from its sheer luxury and pampering, its location is an excellent base for explorations to the ancient temples and breathtaking landscapes further north as well as the vibrant culture of rural central Java, which is in great contrast to the court life of Jogja's aristocracy.

Amanjiwo Resort

Desa Majaksingi, Borobudur, Magelang,
Tel: (62-293) 788-333,
www.amanresorts.com

EAST JAVA

Hotel Tugu Malang

Overnighting at Hotel Tugu Malang is akin to sleeping in a museum-cum-art gallery. The entire resort is influenced by the Baba Peranakan culture, a mixture of Chinese immigrants and native Javanese. Other Tugu hotels are in Bali, Lombok and Blitar, East Java, and each is filled with priceless artworks collected by the owner. If time doesn't permit staying in one of them, at least drop by one of their wonderful eateries and have a look around while you're there.

Jl. Tugu No. 3, Malang,
Tel: (62-341) 363-891, www.tuguhotels.com

Hotel Majapahit Surabaya

A beautifully restored example of a bygone era, Hotel Majapahit Surabaya was the vision of one of the Armenian Sarkies brothers of the famed Raffles Hotel Singapore, The Strand in Rangoon and The Eastern and Oriental in Penang. Originally constructed in 1910 and later expanded in 1936, stars such as Charlie Chaplin and Paulette Goddard are said to have attended its grand opening. Its Dutch colonial architecture is still elegant today and its staff gracious.

Jl. Tunjungan, Surabaya, Tel: (62-31)
545-4333, www.hotel-majapahit.com

SOUTH BALI

W Retreat & Spa Bali—Seminyak

Hip, colorful, vibrant, trendy and loaded with pizazz, the W Retreat & Spa Bali—Seminyak, set amidst natural attractions, was designed from top to bottom for the young and active. The minute you walk into its open-air lobby you feel alive, and if Bali doesn't have enough adventure for you, its Always® Spa is open 24/7 as is its Sweat® Fitness Center. Despite its glitz, it manages to feel homey, thanks in great part to an excellent staff.

Jl. Petitenget, Seminyak, Tel: (62-361)
473-8106, www.starwoodhotels.com

The Legian Bali

Setting the bar very high for every resort that followed on exclusive Seminyak beach, a prime stretch of golden sand, The Legian Bali was one of the originals and remains an all-time favorite for many Bali visitors today. Every amenity imaginable has been included, from shoreline dining and spa and fitness on its private beach to Blu-Ray DVD player, iPod dock, Apple Video iPods and goose down pillows. Among its many accolades for excellence are several Wine Spectator Awards.

Jl. Kayu Aya, Seminyak Beach, Tel: (63-361) 730-622, wwww.thelegianbali.com

Bulgari Resort Bali

Presenting the ultimate in total luxury and privacy, Bulgari Resort Bali stands regally on a cliff overlooking the Indian Ocean in the remote Uluwatu area of southern Bali. A fusion of Italian design and Balinese craftsmanship, hand-hewn volcanic rocks and local woods bedeck the interiors of secluded villas, as discrete butlers cater to your every whim. The glorious beach below the cliff is accessed only by the resort's inclined elevator. Prepare to be pampered.

Jl. Goa Lempeh, Banjar Dinas Kangin,
Uluwatu, Tel: (62-361) 847-1000,
www.bulgarihotels.com

Four Seasons Resort at Jimbaran Bay
Great for families, at Four Seasons Resort at Jimbaran Bay luxuriate in the privacy of your villa or join the fun on the expansive grounds. Cooking classes include pastry for kids. Take a family class on Balinese massage, cruise to Nusa Penida, or leave the children in the care of trained staff at the kids-only infinity-edge Jacuzzi pool while you indulge in a spa treatment or simply relax. Don't miss the free homemade sorbet poolside in the afternoons.
Jimbaran, Tel: (62-361) 701-010,
www.fourseasons.com

Banyan Tree Ungasan Bali
Designed to evoke serenity and located south of Nusa Dua, Banyan Tree Ungasan Bali is another of the southern peninsula's astonishing cliff-perched resorts, only this one has a unique surprise: the Ju-Ma-Na bar with a Moroccan atmosphere, complete with shisha pipes. The decor also has a more contemporary feel to it than its other ultra-lux resort neighbors, and of course it includes a renowned Banyan Tree Spa, made famous in its Phuket property.
Jl. Melasti, Banjar Kelod, Ungasan,
Tel: (62-361) 300-7000,
www.banyantree.com

CENTRAL BALI
Four Seasons Resort Bali at Sayan
It is difficult to decide which of the many unique aspects of the Conde Nast Traveler's Gold List 2012 Four Seasons Resort Bali at Sayan makes it so charming. Its unique rooftop lily pond that greets you on arrival demands that you pause and gaze. But the way the entire resort hugs the banks of the sacred Ayung River on the outskirts of Ubud, with terraced rice fields and palms on the opposite bank, evokes visions of Eden. And the service, of course, is impeccable.
Sayan, Ubud, Tel: (62-361) 977-577,
www.fourseasons.com

Komaneka at Bisma
In addition to lavishly huge rooms, bathrooms and balconies at this contemporary resort, the views are one of the many things that make Komaneka at Bisma so special. Set beside rice fields and coconut groves bordered by dense jungle, only a short walk from downtown Ubud in the Campuan River valley, there is superb scenery from every room. Rave reviews go to the staff members who, as with the other two Komanekas at Monkey Forest and Tanggayuda, are ever gracious and unassuming.
Jl. Bisma, Ubud, Tel: (62-361) 971-933,
www.komaneka.com

Uma Ubud
A COMO Hotels & Resorts property, Uma Ubud's focus is on healthy living in an atmosphere far enough removed from the center of Ubud to be quietly serene but near enough to it to be accessible. An open-air yoga pavilion, meditation *balé* and amazing spa treatments are only the beginning. Factor in early morning rice field strolls, guided adventure outings and healthful food in its restaurant and the sum is pretty close to nirvana.
Jl. Raya Sanggingan, Banjar Lungsiakan,
Kedewatan, Ubud, (62-361) 972-448,
www.como.bz

Alam Indah
Fans of Ibu Wayan's cooking at Ubud's Cafe Wayan didn't take long to discover Alam Indah when it opened in 1995.

Since then, her family business has expanded to five intimate hotels, a small spa and a handicrafts gallery, but Alam Indah remains the favorite home base in Ubud for many who return time and time again. The focus here is on interacting with nature and Balinese culture, and you'll be warmly welcomed and treated as a member of the extended family.
Desa Nyuhkuning, Ubud,
Tel: (62-361) 974-629,
www.alamindahbali.com

WEST BALI

The Menjangan
A boutique resort-retreat located inside the West Bali National Park, The Menjangan is all about nature, beginning with its lookout tower above the main lodge, which is ideal for bird-watching, and extending to forest trees labeled with scientific names. Revel in horseback riding, trekking and biking on land, and at sea there's yachting, kayaking and, of course, snorkeling and diving at Bali's best sites near Menjangan Island. Be sure to reserve enough time for relaxing and rejuvenating with a massage in the open air while enjoying the sounds of nature that surround the resort.
Jl. Raya Gilimanuk, Singaraja Km 17,
Desa Pajarakan, Tel: (62-362) 94700,
www.themenjangan.com

NORTH BALI

Matahari Beach Resort & Spa
Hardly anyone would expect to find a luxurious five-star resort in northern Bali, one of the island's least visited areas, but the Matahari Beach Resort & Spa, located on a secluded black sand lava beach near Pemuteran, Singaraja, surrounded by national parks and ma-

rine conservation areas, is exactly that. Its many trophies include Green Hotel, Most Beautiful Spa, Tranquility from renowned Relais & Chateaux, Best Garden and multiple Tri Hita Karana tourism awards denoting its commitment to promoting Balinese culture in harmony with nature. What else needs to be said?
Jl. Raya Seririt-Gilimanuk, Pemuteran,
Tel: (62-362) 92312,
http://matahari-beach-resort.com

LOMBOK

Qunci Villas
The terms 'chic', 'Zen' and 'hip' are all used to describe Qunci Villas on Lombok's Mangsit beach, but they fail to fully describe how wonderful this resort really is. Being away from oft-crowded Senggigi beach in a private little cove is a big bonus, and whether you opt for one of the elegant rooms or the luxurious villas, the price is nearly half what you'd pay elsewhere for similar excellence. All these factors add up to a perfect holiday away from reality.
Jl. Raya Mangsit, Tel: (62-370) 693-800,
http://quncivillas.com

Tugu Lombok Sire Beach
Another exquisite collection of art and antiques to live among and enjoy, unlike its sister property in Malang, eastern Java, the Tugu Lombok Sire Beach focuses on the antiquities of the romantic *Mahabharata* epic that existed long before invaders reached the island. Its decor is an eclectic blend of bold colors and treasures. Yoga, meditation and an indoor/outdoor spa will relax and restore, and Lombok's best golf course is nearby.
Sigar Penjalin village, Tanjung,
Tel: (62-370) 612-0111, www.tuguhotels.com

INDONESIA'S BEST FOODS & RESTAURANTS

Indonesian food varies from region to region, dependant on availability of ingredients, local traditions of combining spices, religious mores, and influences brought by foreign merchants during the heyday of its maritime trade centuries ago. For example, the curries used in Sumatran cuisine indisputably arrived from India and the Middle East, and the smorgasbord-style *rijsttafel* was invented by the Dutch, who also introduced bread, cheeses and pancakes, while Chinese restaurants are ubiquitous. White rice is the staple of all meals in the western part of the country, but in the drier eastern areas the main carbohydrates are sago, cassava, sweet potatoes and corn.

Chicken and fish are the major meat sources, usually taken as a side dish rather than a main course. Due to religious constraints, primarily Muslim, Javanese eateries do not serve pork, and their mainly Hindu-Balinese neighbors shun beef. Seafood is abundant in all coastal areas and is especially delicious served *bakar* (grilled over a charcoal fire). Vegetables usually consist of seasonal local produce, and fresh tropical fruits are abundant.

With its long history as a major spice producer, endemic nutmeg and mace, cloves and galangal are often combined with other ingredients introduced by early traders: black pepper, turmeric, lemongrass, shallots and cinnamon from India, and garlic, ginger and green onions from China.

Many dishes are accompanied by *sambal*, a spicy hot condiment based on chili peppers. Peanuts are also frequently used as a garnish or in a sauce that includes savory, sweet, sour and spicy elements. Thin coconut milk is used in soups and a thicker version laces stews or desserts. Another Indonesian favorite flavoring is

Ayam penyet with sambal

Spicy satay

kecap manis, soy sauce sweetened with palm sugar, used as a meat marinade, as a condiment and in stews.

Away from city centers, the only option is usually regional food, but several dishes are found on every menu throughout Indonesia: *nasi goreng* (fried rice), *mie goreng* (fried noodles), *nasi campur* (a complete meal with rice, a vegetable and a meat, usually chicken), *soto* (soup), many varieties of *sate* (satay, skewered meat) and Chinese food.

JAVA

Favorite Sundanese dishes from western Java include *ikan mas bakar* or *goreng* (golden carp, either grilled or fried), *pepes* (fish or chicken wrapped in a banana leaf and steamed or grilled), oxtail soup and *karedok*, a salad made with firm vegetables in a spicy sauce.

Central Javanese cuisine tends to be sweeter than that found in western or eastern Java. In Jogja, the specialty is *gudeg*, a stew of young jackfruit simmered in coconut milk and spices served with chicken, egg or tofu and rice, and *ayam goreng*, Javanese-style fried chicken. Other central Java specialties include *pecel* (spinach or long beans and bean sprouts with peanut sauce), *lotek* (vegetables and pressed rice served with peanut sauce), *opor ayam* (braised chicken in coconut sauce) and *nasi liwet* (rice cooked in coconut milk).

The cuisine of eastern Java is similar to that of central Java, but less sweet and not as spicy. *Rawon* (darkened beef stew) is a particular favorite. Exceptions are Madura Island dishes, such as *soto madura* (beef soup), found throughout Java, which are saltier than eastern Java foods.

BALI

For the Balinese, food is grouped into two categories: regular meals and ceremonial dishes that take a very long time to prepare. Fortunately for them and for the world, many of these special foods are now available in *warung* (roadside eateries) found throughout the island.

Babi guling (spit-roasted pig) ranks among the islanders' favorites during rituals, perhaps followed by *lawar*, an interesting combination of minced meat, grated coconut, vegetables, spices and pigs' blood. *Sate lilit* is also popular, but rather than the chunks of meat found in the satay of other islands, chicken, beef, goat, duck or fish are pounded into a smooth mixture with grated coconut as a binder before grilling or frying the skewered meat. Duck is used more often in Balinese cooking than elsewhere in Indonesia, and includes the tasty *bebek goreng* (fried duck) and *betutu*, grilled spicy duck wrapped in banana leaves and steamed. Generally, Balinese cuisine is saltier than that of other regions and is often compared to Padang food for its extreme spiciness. In tourist areas the fire has been turned down for foreign palates in almost every eatery to the point that it is now difficult to find authentic Balinese food in those regions.

LOMBOK

In western Lombok, where there is a large population of Balinese, many of the same dishes found on Bali are served in eateries here. However, as Lombok's native Sasak people are primarily Muslim, no pork is served.

It is oddly appropriate that the traditional Sasak cuisine of Lombok (which means 'chili') is spicy hot. *Ayam taliwang*, which is roasted chicken served with a peanut, tomato and lime sauce laced with chilies, is recognized throughout Indonesia as a Lombok dish. Other well-known tongue burners are dishes made with *plecing*, a spicy sauce of chilies, shrimp paste and tomatoes, such as *kangkung plecing*, cooked water spinach. Whether imitating Bali's *sate lilit* or not, Lombok's *sate pusut* is equally well known; it comprises a minced meat and coconut milk mixture flavored with garlic and other spices. The red snapper (*kakap*) *sate pusut* dipped in sweet soy bean sauce (*kecap manis*) is especially tasty.

SUMATRA

The Batak of northern Sumatra favor some unusual dishes, such as *saksang*, roasted pork served with a spicy sauce made of pig's blood. Watch out for dog meat served for special occasions. A Medan specialty is *kambing kurma*, lamb in curry sauce.

Western Sumatra is known for its spicy Padang food which can be found at *rumah makan Padang* (Padang eating houses), also called *rumah makan Minangkabau*, throughout Indonesia. It is fiery hot and not for the faint of heart. Still hot, but fabulously delicious is west Sumatra's famous *rendang*, originally buffalo meat but often beef simmered in coconut milk and spices until the meat is tender. Also try their *dendeng balado* (crispy beef with red chilies) and boiled egg in curry or *gulai kepala kakap*, red snapper fish-head curry.

SULAWESI

The Minahasan of northern Sulawesi favor meats of all kinds, including rats, bats and dogs, making it a good idea for the squeamish to inquire about ingredients before ordering. Like the Balinese, the primarily Christian Minahasan also eat a lot of pork. *Babi putar* (a whole young pig spit-roasted over charcoals) is a must at weddings and birthday celebrations. *Rica-rica* is an oily chili sauce spiced with red onions and is used on fried or grilled fish and chicken. *Sayur bunga pepaya* (stir-fried papaya flower) is among the favorite vegetable side dishes.

Makassar, in southern Sulawesi, has a reputation for a wide variety of local dishes, and fresh grilled seafood is aplenty, served with several varieties of *sambal*, particularly in coastal areas. *Coto Makassar* (spicy soup with cow's innards and brain) and *sop konro* (grilled rib soup) are served in almost every local restaurant in Makassar.

The eateries listed on pages 95–6 are the best restaurants in their cities serving authentic regional cuisines, and don't be surprised that some of them are franchises or have more than one location. Finding 'real' Indonesian food often requires getting off the beaten tourist track, and a sign of their excellence in quality is the crowds of Indonesians who frequent them.

Dendeng balado

Jakarta Restaurants

Practically all the regional cuisines from throughout Indonesia can be found in Jakarta, but especially recommended are:

PAYON, Jl. Kemang Raya No. 17, Tel: (62-21) 719-4826. Excellent central, western and eastern Javanese cuisine set in a series of buildings surrounded by gardens reminiscent of a traditional village.

VOC GALANGAN CAFE & RESTO, Jl. Kakap No. 1, Tel: (62-21) 667-0981. Indonesian and Dutch-Indonesian fusion cuisine served in a beautifully restored 17th-century Dutch warehouse or outdoors on the adjoining terrace. Like stepping back in time.

GARUDA, Jl. Hayam Wuruk No. 100, Tel: (62-21) 626-2914. One of several outlets serving tasty Padang food at great prices, getting outstanding reviews for consistently good quality. Try one of the spicy curries.

SATE KHAS SENAYAN, Jl. Kebon Sirih Raya 31A, Tel: (62-21) 326-238. Delicious regional Indonesian dishes, specializing in *sate* (satay); has outlets in other locations. Heartily recommended is the moist, tender *sate ayam* (chicken satay).

OASIS, Jl. Raden Saleh No. 47, Tel: (62-21) 315-0646, www.oasis-restaurant.co.id. A long-time Jakarta landmark and the place to go for elegantly served *rijsttafel*. The setting is ideal for a wander back in time: a two-story mansion that was the private residence of a Dutch East Indies plantation owner.

BUMBU DESA, Jl. Cikini Raya No. 72, Tel: (62-21) 390-4747. A chain of restaurants serving a wide range of traditional Sundanese dishes. The crispy fried gurame fish is particularly favored.

Bandung Restaurants
KAMPUNG DAUN CULTURE GALLERY & CAFE, Jl. Sersan Bajuri Km 4.7 No. 88 RRI, Tel: (62-22) 278-7915. Popular for its Sundanese cuisine served in gazebos set atop a hill overlooking the city. Great atmosphere, excellent food and service, and usually crowded.

Puncak Restaurants
PUNCAK PASS RESORT, Jl. Raya Puncak, Cianjur, Tel: (62-263) 512-503. www. puncakpassresort.com. Established in 1928, the resort has been widely known for its Dutch dishes since it was first established to cater to colonial holiday-makers. Try the *poffertjes*, *kroket* and *bitterballen*.

Jogja Restaurants
SASANTI RESTAURANT & GALLERY, Jl. Palagan Tentara Pelajar No. 52A, Tel: (62-274) 866-345, www.sasantirestaurant.com. Authentic Javanese recipes using the finest ingredients, such as Wagyu beef. Covered or garden dining in a fusion of Javanese, Balinese and Western architecture made from recycled materials. Also has an excellent Western menu.

THE HOUSE OF RAMINTEN, Jl. FM Noto No. 7, Kota Baru, Tel: (62-274) 586-928. Originally selling only *jamu*, traditional herbal drinks, it became so popular that a Javanese menu was added, served by waiters in traditional attire. A favorite of students, so expect crowds.

JALAN KULINER, Jl. Palagan Tentara Pelajar. The road north of Hyatt Regency Yogyakarta and streets branching off of it is lined with small restaurants and cafes specializing in seafood, Balinese and Javanese cuisine.

Malang Restaurants

TOKO OEN, Jl. Basuki Rachmat 5, Tel: (62-341) 364-052. A classic eatery that began by serving ice cream and morphed into serving Dutch and Indonesian food. Its old Dutch building, decorated with stained-glass windows and period furniture, coupled with traditionally attired waiters suits its menu to a tee. There is another Toko Oen in Semarang, central Java.

Bali Restaurants

BUMBU BALI RESTAURANT & COOKING SCHOOL, Jl. Pratama, Tanjung Benoa, Tel: (62-361) 774-502, www.balifoods.com. Exquisitely prepared authentic Balinese and other regional cuisines that even the Balinese rave about. The owner has authored several Balinese cookbooks and also offers cooking classes. There is now a second location and a Pasar Malam market restaurant.

JIMBARAN BEACH, A number of al fresco restaurants line the beach for fresh seafood prepared to customers' orders. All are usually crowded at sunset.

BEBEK BENGIL (Dirty Duck Diner), Jl. Hanoman, Padang Tegal, Ubud, Tel: (62-361) 975-489, www.bebekbengil.com. Named for the first guests that arrived from an adjoining rice field, this is one of the few places that serves delicious *bebek goreng* (crispy fried duck) without a 24-hour advance notice.

CAFE WAYAN, Jl. Monkey Forest, Ubud, Tel: (62-361) 975-447, www.alamindah-bali.com. A perennial favorite for Balinese (and Western) food, try the Sunday evening Balinese buffet for a variety of traditional dishes. Ibu Wayan's daughter, also an excellent chef, offers Balinese cooking classes at her restaurant, Laka Leke, on the opposite side of the Monkey Forest.

CASA LUNA RESTAURANT, Jl. Raya, Ubud, Tel: (62-361) 977-409, www.casalunabali.com. The cafe primarily attracts foreign tourists for its Western food and bakery, but it also has a cooking school orchestrated by the owner and the author of a Balinese cookbook.

IBU OKA'S WARUNG BABI GULING, Jl. Suweta/Tegal Sari No. 2 Ubud, Tel: (62-361) 976-345. Arguably the best *babi guling* (roast suckling pig) in Bali, spiced and spit-roasted for five hours over an open fire using the same recipe handed down from the owner's parents-in-law. Get there early to get a seat. Opens 11 am, closes mid-afternoon.

MOZAIC RESTAURANT GASTRONOMIQUE, Jl. Raya Sanggingan, Ubud, Tel: (62-361) 975-768, www.mozaic-bali.com. Although it doesn't serve regional cuisine (think Modern French with Balinese flavors), no list of Indonesia's best restaurants is complete without award-winning Mozaic. Opens at 6 pm. Reservations are strongly recommended.

Cafe Wayan Balinese buffet

INDONESIA'S BEST SHOPPING

JAKARTA

Shopaholics will swoon with delight over cosmopolitan Jakarta's extensive browsing and buying options. Its many upper echelon malls lure buyers with international branded designer goods, some of the best food in the city, entertainment, cinemas, kids' play sections and relief from the sun, rain and traffic.

Sudirman/Thamrin Business District

One of Southeast Asia's largest upscale shopping centers, **Grand Indonesia Shopping Town** is a two-building complex connected by a skywalk located behind Hotel Indonesia Kempinski in the center of the Sudirman/Thamrin Business District. Directly across the street and connected to the Grand Hyatt is the luxurious **Plaza Indonesia**. A walkway through this lush compound leads to **fX Lifestyle X'nter**, filled to the brim with entertainment options and shops. On the opposite side of the street, about a 10-minute walk away, is **Sarinah** department store, the city's first department store, whose three floors dedicated to Indonesian-made products feature batik, souvenirs, art, handicrafts and packaged food items.

If the urge to shop has not yet abated, at the southern end of Jl. Sudirman where it meets Jl. Asia-Afrika are **Senayan City** and **Plaza Senayan**, two large lifestyle and entertainment centers carrying international brands, Indonesian designers' boutiques, eateries, bars, cinemas, spas and fitness centers.

South Jakarta

For another enormous range of Indonesian batik and traditional arts and crafts, visit **Pasaraya** on Jl. Iskandarsyah in Blok M, south Jakarta. The complex also includes cafes, movie theaters, a bowling center and wellness facilities.

Heading further south is **Kemang**, once merely an affluent residential neighborhood and now the home of many of Jakarta's trendiest fashion boutiques, interior designers, nearly 150 art galleries, and around 160 restaurants, cafes, bars and nightclubs. Check local calendars of events for exhibitions and festivals, as there is always something going on here in addition to shopping.

BANDUNG

Bandung is well known for its plethora of factory outlets selling overruns and slightly defective international brand fashions, accessories and bed and bath. Check items carefully before buying as they cannot be returned, and watch out for fake items, which do creep in. There are many shops in the Dago, Sukajadi, Jl. Riau and Dr Otten areas, and especially recommended are **DSE** (Dago Stock Ekspo, Jl. Ir. H. Djuanda No. 52), **Export Station** (Jl. Sumatera No. 24-30), **FOS Clothing** (Jl. Dr Otten No. 6), **Rich & Famous** (Jl. Dago No. 14), **Rival** (Jl. Dr Abdul Rivai No. 11) and **Rumah Mode** (Jl. Setiabudhi No. 41F).

'**Jeans Street**' (Jl. Cihampelas) is filled with outlets selling denim jeans, and look for shoes on Jl. Cibaduyut.

YOGYAKARTA

The villages surrounding Jogja are home to several thousand expert craftsmen and women fashioning central Java's finest batik, silver jewelry, leather goods,

Balinese painter

BALI
Seminyak

Jl. Raya Seminyak and Jl. Laksmana in upmarket Seminyak have blossomed into a haven for boutique shoppers, who can find export quality fashions for the whole family, home interiors, ceramics and jewelry. For fashions, visit **Animale**, **By The Sea**, **Mama and Leon**, **Paul Ropp** and **Uluwatu**, to name a few. Most have branches in other locations.

Jimbaran

Bali's best, and priciest, ceramic dinnerware and home accessories, along with a cafe and classes, are those made by **Jenggala Keramik** (Jl. Uluwatu II, Jimbaran, Tel: (62-361) 703-310, www.jenggala-bali.com).

On the road to Ubud

Handicraft lovers will find entire villages dedicated to a single art form on the road to Ubud, with shops lining both sides of the road: **Batubulan** for stone carving; **Mas** for wood carvings and masks; and **Celuk** for silver jewelry. For one-stop shopping for these and more, visit **Pasar Seni** in Sukawati.

For high quality dance masks, the most accomplished carvers are Ida Bagus Anom in Mas (next to the football field), whose innovative designs are everywhere in Bali, and Ida Bagus Alit in Lod Tunduh, just south of the junction at Mas and Lod Tunduh. Other preeminent mask makers in the area are: in

pottery, natural fiber home accessories and wood carvings, many of export quality. A wide range of these products are available at Jogja's 'downtown' traditional market, **Pasar Beringharjo**, on Jl. Malioboro, where there are also kiosks lining both sides of the street selling souvenir quality goods.

Better yet, spend a day in the countryside buying directly from the craftsmen in their village workshops and seeing many of the wares being made. For pottery tableware and home accessories, visit **Pundong** village, 8 km south of Jogja, and **Kasongan** village, 10 km south of Jogja. Renowned for its silver jewelry, **Kota Gede** village is fun to visit via *andong* (horse-drawn carriage) from Jl. Malioboro.

The best *batik tulis* (hand-drawn batik) can be found at **Afif Syakur Batik** (Jl. Pendega Marta No. 37A, Tel: (62-274) 589-914, 580-665), **Bixa Batik Studio and Gallery** (Pengok PJKA GK 1/7/43F, Tel: (62-274) 546-545), **Gallery Batik Jawa** (Mustakaweni Hotel, Jl. AM Sanghaji No. 72, Tel: (62-274) 515-268), and stunning, collectible contemporary batik at **Brahma Tirta Sari Studio** (Desa Tegal Cerme Kd. V, RT 08/RW 14, Banguntapan, south Jogja, Tel: (62-274) 377-881, www.brahmatirtasari.com).

Jenggala Keramic

Singapadu, I Wayan Tangguh, Cokorda Raka Tisnu and I Wayan Tedun; and in Mas, Ida Bagus Oka and I Wayan Muka.

Belaga village near Blahbatuh specializes in tables, chairs and other furniture made of attractive spotted bamboo. Next door is Bona, with a large bamboo and rattan furniture collection.

Ubud

Local artists sell their work at shops and kiosks along every street, and Ubud's art galleries feature all genres ranging from the Young Artists group to Pop, Macro Art and Magic Realism. For reputable fine art sales, visit:

ARMA (Agung Rai Museum of Art) Art Gallery, Jl. Cokorda Rai Pudak, Tel: (62-361) 976-559, www.armamuseum.com. Museum quality paintings.

GAYA FUSION ART SPACE, Jl. Raya Sayan, Sayan, Tel: (62-361) 979-253, 979-252, www.gayafusion.com. Features avant garde and contemporary art.

HANNA ARTSPACE, Jl. Raya Pengosekan, Peliatan, Tel: (62-361) 978-216. Located on the grounds of the Pertamina petrol station, features young and upcoming artists.

KOMANEKA FINE ART GALLERY, Jl. Monkey Forest, Tel: (62-361) 976-090, www.komaneka.com. Revolving exhibitions of contemporary artists.

NEKA ART GALLERY, Jl. Raya Ubud (opposite the post office), Tel: (62-361) 975-034. The gallery outlet of the respected Neka Museum.

RIO HELMI PHOTOGRAPHY, Jl. Suweta No. 5, Tel: (62-361) 972-304, www.riohelmi.

Balinese handicrafts

com. Stunning images of his homeland by renowned Indonesian photographer Rio Helmi. His gallery features his photographs as well as prints.

SENIWATI GALLERY OF ART BY WOMEN, Jl. Sriwidari 2B, Tel: (62-361) 975-485, www.seniwatigallery.com. Supports little-recognized female Balinese artists.

TONY RAKA GALLERY, Jl. Raya Mas No. 86, Mas village, Tel: (62-361) 781-6785, www.tonyrakaartgallery.com. An innovative art gallery featuring fresh and often wacky art. For lower prices on wooden handicrafts in all imaginable sizes, shapes and colors, head up the hill to Tegallalang, Pujung and Sebatu villages, all northeast of Ubud. In these crafts villages are a bewildering number of shops, mostly for export purposes.

BOJOG GALLERY, across from the football field on Jl. Monkey Forest, Tel: (62-361) 971-001. Two stories of antique furniture, textiles, puppets, masks, wood carvings and more from throughout Indonesia.

CELENG GALLERY, Jl. Raya Lungsiakan, Kedewatan, Tel: (62-361) 898-9488, Mobile: 0811-396-860. Antique furniture, stone carvings and ritual artifacts.

HANANTO LLOYD, Jl. Raya Sayan, Tel: (62-361) 742-9337, www.hanantolloyd.com. Home decor, antiques, designer jewelry and interior design.

KULUK GALLERY, Jl. Raya Lungsiakan, Kedewatan, Tel: (62-361) 975-833. Indonesian art and antiques, specializing in museum quality ritual artifacts and antique textiles and jewelry.

MURNI'S WARUNG SHOP, at Murni's Warung, Jl Raya Ubud, beside the Campuan bridge, Tel: (62-361) 972-146, www.murnis.com. Traditional arts and crafts from all over the archipelago.

PASAR UBUD (Ubud traditional market), Jl. Raya Ubud, Central Ubud. Crafts, household items, sarongs, spices. Also a good selection of silver jewelry, carvings, paintings, textiles, bedcovers, unusual souvenirs, aromatherapy oils and incense. Bargain like mad.

TEGUN FOLK ART GALLERY, Jl. Hanoman 44, Padangtegal, Tel: (62-361) 970-581, www.tegun.com. Unique and well-selected gifts, keepsakes and other paraphernalia gathered from all over the archipelago.

TOKO EAST, Jl. Raya Ubud, Tel: (62-361) 978-306, www.dekco.com. Contemporary Indonesian exterior and interior homewares. Features stoneware, ceramics, table top accessories, unique decorative items and garden lamps.

Silver & Gold Jewelry

For fabulous silver and gold jewelry with or without gemstones, **Jean Francois** (Jl. Raya No. 7, www.if-f.com), **Runa House of Design and Museum** (Lod Tunduh), and **Treasures** (Jl. Raya Ubud, next door

Balinese mask

to Ary's) feature original designs created by Bali's best artisans.

Textiles

The finest handwoven textiles from across the archipelago, with each island and village featuring unique motifs and colors, are displayed and sold at **Threads of Life** (Jl. Kajeng 24, www.threadsoflife.com), a gallery and non-profit organization dedicated to preserving weaving and empowering women.

LOMBOK

Lombok is known for its textiles, pottery and basketry. Traditional textiles are woven by hand in **Sukarare** (*tenun Lombok*), **Pujung** (*kain lambung*), **Purbasari** (*kain Purbasari*), **Balimurti** (the sacred *beberut* cloth) and **Pringgasela** villages. **Banyumulek**, **Masbagik** and **Penujak** villages all produce export quality pottery, each with unique motifs. Finely woven rattan and grass baskets are sold at **Pasar Mandalika** near the Sweta bus terminal and at **Pasar Cakranegara**, west of Pura Meru temple.

INDONESIA'S HIPPEST NIGHTLIFE

Nightlife in Indonesia is primarily limited to bars in large-city international hotels. The exceptions to the rule, however, are Jakarta, southern Bali and Ubud. While Bali is little affected by the Muslim fasting month, note that nightlife on Java usually remain open but might close earlier than usual. In that event, partygoers head to the big hotel bars, which are allowed to remain open for tourists.

JAKARTA

Jakarta rocks at night and services clientele ranging from the beer-swilling types to the beautiful people who migrate from club to club to be seen. International DJs, music of all genres, pulsating dance floors and, in some places, rampant naughtiness rule. The action begins with after-work happy hours and progresses into the wee hours. Note that prostitution and drugs (possession of which is punishable by death) do creep into the scene, and both are illegal.

Also check schedules upon arrival for global rock star concerts, international film and jazz festivals and performances by one of Jakarta's three symphony orchestras.

DRAGONFLY, Graha BIP, Jl. Jend. Gatot Subroto No. 23, Tel: (62-21) 520-6789, www.ismaya.com. A long-time favorite with models and elites for its rotating international DJs playing the coolest tracks.

IMMIGRANT BAR, Plaza Indonesia, 6th Floor #E02-03, Tel: (62-21) 3983-8257. Popular with upmarket executives and expats,

The Stadium nightclub

this club is a bit more sophisticated than the haunts frequented by the younger crowd. Great skyline view of the city

RED SQUARE JAKARTA, Senayan Plaza Arcadia, Unit X210-211, Jl. New Delhi No. 9, Pintu 1, Tel: (62-21) 5790-1281, www. redsquarejakarta.com. 'The' expat haven specializing in vodka cocktails, shots, martinis and infusions in an astonishing array of flavors. Booking a table in advance on weekends is almost essential.

STADIUM, Jl. Hayam Wuruk 111, Tel: (62-21) 626-3323, www.stadiumjakarta.com. Without a doubt, the city's hottest club, with four floors of food, drink and disco delight. Capacity 5,000 hardy partiers.

X2 CLUB, Plaza Senayan, 4th & 5th floors, Senayan Square Complex, Jl. Asia-Afrika No. 8, Tel: (62-21) 572-5559. Four dancing areas on two floors for hip-hop and R&B enthusiasts, progressive house music lovers, an older crowd of expats and executives, and a VIP room. Expect huge crowds.

BLACKCAT JAZZ AND BLUES CLUB, Plaza Senayan Arcadia, Unit X 208-209, Jl. New Delhi No. 9, Pintu 1, Tel: (62-21) 5790-1264, www.blackcatjakarta.com. Live jazz and blues bands and piano music in a classy, upscale atmosphere. Check website for performance schedules. Cajun/Creole menu, friendly staff and attentive service.

CAFE BATAVIA BAR, Fatahillah Square, Jl. Pintu Besar Utara 14, Kota, Jakarta, Tel: (62-21) 691-5531. Housed in a 19th-century Dutch building and crammed to the rafters with antiques, movie star photos and memorabilia, this place

exudes atmosphere. Especially nice at night overlooking the old square.

Kemang

At night, many of the young and trendy head to Kemang, a well-to-do neighborhood south of the city center. Jl. Kemang Raya, the main street that is lined with shops, restaurants, cafes, bars and pubs, is too long to walk from one end to another, so by driving by and having a look first before parking, pub crawling in this area becomes more doable. Favorite nightlife are:

BEER GARDEN KEMANG, Jl. Benda No. 7, Tel: (62-21) 789-1145. An easy-going garden setting (with retractable roof in case of rain) featuring imported and unusual beers. Casual and comfortable. Acoustic music some nights.

ELBOW ROOM, Jl. Kemang Raya No. 24A, Tel: (62-21) 719-4274. Interesting menu includes imported wines and beers and European food, favored by a more mature crowd. Music is relaxing and soft enough to encourage conversations.

MURPHY'S IRISH PUB & RESTAURANT, Jl. Kemang Raya No. 11, Tel: (62-21) 718-3382, www.murphysjakarta.com. Owned by an Irish expat, featuring great food and beer (Irish, of course), nightly music, and sports on a large plasma screen.

SHY ROOFTOP KEMANG, The Papilion, Level 5, Jl. Kemang Raya No. 45AA, Tel: (62-21) 719-9921. An elegant bar above a French restaurant attracting a slightly older crowd than the normal Kemang student and rich kids' hangouts. Atmosphere is comfortable and live acoustic music not ear-splittingly loud.

BALI

Kuta's legendary nightlife begins with sundowners anywhere along the beach, later migrating inland, where it generally revolves around ear-splitting music geared to young, rambunctious party-goers. After dinner, a more sophisticated crowd heads to Seminyak, where many lounges begin hopping around 11 pm, with the real action taking place from 2 am onwards. Be aware that in Seminyak, it's best to dress 'smart casual'. The crowds follow the best DJs, so ask locally and check websites to see what's going on before heading out.

As the hippest places of the moment come and go with amazing speed, the listings below are the tried and true lounges and bars that have withstood the test of time and remain popular today:

HARD ROCK CAFE, Jl. Pantai Kuta, Kuta, Tel: (62-361) 755-661, www.hardrock.com. The cafe and its decor are legendary, of course, but not to be overlooked is that young crowds flock here at night to hear live music, which frequently includes well-known Indonesian stars.

HU'U BAR & BABA'S RESTAURANT, Jl. Petit-enget, Seminyak, Tel: (62-361) 473-6576, http://huubali.com. What began only as a cool hangout place has over the years evolved into an elegant dining venue that its name doesn't justify. What hasn't changed is the nighttime scene, beginning with elaborate pre-dinner cocktails and exciting DJs spinning tunes until dawn.

KU DE TA, Jl. Kayu Aya No. 9, Seminyak, Tel: (62-361) 736-969, www.kudeta.net. Stands in a class by itself as a sophisticated all-day fine dining restaurant,

family-oriented beach club and sunset cocktail spot. After hours, international performers rock in the VIP Lounge. Check the website for strict dress code rules.

SKY GARDEN LOUNGE, 61 Legian Entertainment Complex, Jl. Legian, Kuta, http://61legian.com. A rooftop bistro-lounge where the fun never stops. Check their website for a sneak peek at what's happening during your visit.

Ubud

JAZZ CAFE, Jl. Sukma, Tel: (62-361) 976-4594, http://jazzcafebali.com. No question about it, this is Ubud's best hangout for music. Jazz, blues, Latin, funk, soul and world music played nightly except Mondays. Reservations are recommended. There are free pick-ups from hotels in the Ubud area or from its sister establishment, **Laughing Buddha Bar**, on Jl. Monkey Forest.

Hu'u Bar & Baba's Restaurant

BEST SPAS & HEALTH RETREATS

All five-star hotels in major cities and tourist areas throughout Indonesia have invested heavily in exquisite day spas featuring massages, scrubs, facials and hair treatments, and many of them are excellent. However, in this chapter the focus is on resorts and centers whose sole purpose is healthy lifestyles and wellness rather than on general tourism. For obvious reasons, the best retreats outside the hotels are in scenic rural areas where there are no street names or addresses. Check websites for maps and directions; better still, arrange a pick-up service when booking your reservations.

JAVA

Martha Tilaar Salon Day Spas
The vision of an Indonesian woman whose small line of natural beauty products blossomed into international distribution, a chain of spas, shops and beauty schools, Martha Tilaar Salon Day Spas are synonymous with interior as well as exterior beauty throughout the cycle of life. Its dozens of salons pamper women with beauty and body treatments delivered by therapists trained by specialists in Bali as part of a women's empowerment program. Expect gentle, discreet and elegant service at any of the Martha Tilaar Salon Day Spas and emerge feeling like Javanese royalty. *Visit www.marthatilaarspa.com for locations in Java, Bali, Sumatra and Kalimantan.*

MesaStila Wellness Retreat
Surrounded by a working coffee plantation and overwhelming natural beauty in the hills three hours north of Jogja, MesaStila Wellness Retreat's menu includes one-day quick escapes for core body conditioning with TRX or reflexology and a facial. Or spend several days cleansing, destressing, recharging or managing fitness and weight. Recipient of the 2012 Best Luxury Destination Spa in Indonesia and Green Hotel Awards, it has the only Turkish Hammam spa in Indonesia. Meditation and Indonesia's Pencak Silat martial arts are coupled with traditional Javanese therapeutic

Martha Tilaar Salon Day Spa

herbal drinks and healthy cuisine for additional benefits.

Magelang, Central Java,
Tel: (62-298) 596-333,
www.mesahotelsandresorts.com

CENTRAL BALI

Bali, considered a holistic, deeply healing destination, is a haven for spa and wellness retreat seekers, particularly in Ubud where there are general and specialist day and overnight centers for nearly every focus, including Balinese astrology, Reiki, traditional healing, psychic and spiritual guidance, and natural medicine. The resorts and centers named here each have a particular vision and are the best in their fields.

Bagus Jati
One of the few Indonesian health and well-being resorts that includes Ayurvedic on its menu, the treatments at Bagus Jati focus on achieving balance of the three Doshas through a series of massages using specifically formulated herbs and oils and can be combined with yoga and meditation therapies. Detox programs can be five or ten nights and include consultation by a doctor, counseling, acupuncture and herbal medicine, complemented by massages. There are also optional jungle treks and village visits. Healthy cooking classes are available to guests in weight management programs.

Banjar Jati, Desa Sebatu, Kecamatan
Tegallalang, Tel: (62-361) 901-1888,
www.bagusjati.com

COMO Shambhala Estate
Awarded the 2012 Conde Nast Traveler Readers' Spa Awards' 'Top 3 Best Spa Retreats', COMO Shambhala Estate also features Ayurvedic among its wellness programs, which are rounded out with cleansing, fitness, stress management and rejuvenation packages. Retreats are led by visiting masters and usually include learning seminars as well as practice and appropriate therapies. Complimentary daily activities include yoga classes and guided walks. As with all COMO properties, the estate supports local communities with a special focus on women.

Banjar Begawan, Desa Melinggih Kelod,
Payangan, Gianyar, Tel: (62-361) 978-888,
www.cse.como.bz

Fivelements, Puri Ahimsa Healing Center
With multiple awards under its belt, including one recognizing its outstanding eco-sensitivity in building design and several in luxury spa categories, Fivelements, Puri Ahimsa Healing Center leads the pack in uniqueness and exclusivity. Being one with nature takes on a new meaning here through the application of holistic Balinese-Hindu philosophies, therapies and self awareness techniques focused on how internal and external forces, working together, unite with the Universe. Experience healing through water therapy, detoxify, indulge in products made in its own Laboratorium, and meditate in its serene sacred spaces.

Banjar Baturning, Mambai, Bali,
Tel: (62-361) 469-206,
http://fivelements.org

Maya Ubud Resort & Spa
Spa at Maya at Maya Ubud Resort & Spa prides itself on its sumptuousness and inspired service enmeshed with environmental responsibility. Another of the Ubud area's multi-award winners

Fivelements, Puri Ahimsa Healing Center

for luxury and hospitality, its day spa half-day packages for men and women are designed to recharge and rejuvenate with morning yoga sessions followed by massage, facial, body scrub or reflexology. Alternatively, spend the whole day beginning with a guided cultural escapade through verdant rice fields to experience village life. Then participate in a cooking class and lunch before indulging in spa pampering in the afternoon.

Jl. Gunung Sari Peliatan, Ubud,
Tel: (62-361) 977-888,
http://mayaubud.com

NORTH BALI

Gaia-Oasis Retreat Center

Set in a little-traveled area north of Mt Batur, the Gaia-Oasis Retreat Center is a peaceful sanctuary far away from the tourist crowds. Owned communally by members following a vision of working with kindred spirits who contribute individual skills toward a common goal, it is a gathering place for those seeking tranquility. Take a break from life's routines to stay awhile in either the retreat's mountain sanctuary or its beach bungalows, attend healing and mind/body awareness classes, seminars or exercise programs, or simply relax and meditate in your own way. Let Bali's grace enchant you.

Dusun Tegal Sumaga, Tejakula, North Bali, Tel: (62-362) 343-6304,
www.gaia-oasis.com

ShangriLa Oceanside Retreat & Spa

Owned by a husband and wife team who are both authors and seminar leaders, the ShangriLa Oceanside Retreat & Spa began as the couple's private spiritual haven and gradually expanded to include pampering guests. Relax in the spa with soul- and body-nurturing treatments, including scrubs, massages, reflexology and facials. Or stay longer and develop a detox or wellness program with your personal counselor. Unique to the ShangriLa is its Sound Table, using tuning forks to manage pain and stimulate the nervous system. All guests are invited to greet each morning with a yoga session in the retreat's Meditation and Yoga Temple.

Bondalem, North Bali,
Tel: (62-362) 705-5669,
http://bali-shangrila.com

INDONESIA'S BEST OUTDOOR ACTIVITIES

With much of Indonesia blanketed with volcanoes, mountains and tropical forests fringed by seas, practically every outdoor activity imaginable is available here. The activities below are the best that the country has to offer, but be aware that some of these destinations might take more than one to five days, not including travel time.

CYCLING

Cycling fever is raging across Indonesia, ranging from Bike2Work clubs in major cities to extreme competitions, such as **Bali Audax** (www.baliaudax.com) and **Sumatra**'s Tour de Singkarak (www.tourdesingkarak.com). In Jakarta, Bike2Work has now grown to roughly 10,000 members. On **Bali**, several companies lead tours of varying dif-ficulty. For customized and challenging itineraries, contact Bali Sport (www.balicycling.com), or for more standard expeditions, see www.baliadventure-tours.com.

DIVING AND SNORKELING

Papua

Raja Ampat in far Western Papua is perhaps the world's premier dive site. Even though getting there isn't swift or easy, intrepid adventurers will be rewarded several times over for their efforts (Papua Diving, www.papua-diving.com).

Nusa Tenggara

Diving in **Komodo National Park** (page 23) should be arranged in advance. In addition to dive safaris, some specialists also offer liveaboards and courses (Dive Komodo, www.divekomodo.com; CN Dive, http://cndivekomodo.com, both in Labuan Bajo, Flores).

  Alor, in eastern Nusa Tenggara, is best known for its magnificent muck diving and schooling orcas (Dive Alor Dive, www.divealordive.com).

Diving

Sulawesi

Bunaken National Park (page 25) is northern Sulawesi's best-known dive spot. To organize your dive holiday, select any one of the conservation-oriented members of the North Sulawesi Watersports Association (www.divenorth-sulawesi.com). In southeastern Sulawesi, check out **Wakatobi Marine National Park**, the island's newest dive mecca (Patuna Resort Wakatobi, www.patuna-resortwakatobi.com).

Lombok

On the **Gili Islands** (page 22), underwater excursions can be booked on the spot at any of the many dive shops. Recommended are Gili Divers (www.gilidivers.com) and Manta Dive (www.manta-dive.com).

Bali

Bali's best diving is at **Menjangan Island** in West Bali National Park. Extensive reef restoration work has been ongoing for over a decade at **Pemuteran** on the north coast, with Reef Seen Aquatics (www.reefseenbali.com) leading the effort and offering dive tours in both areas. On Bali's east coast, wreck diving at **Tulamben** can be arranged by Eco-Dive Bali in Amed (www.ecodive-bali.com). Off the southeastern coast, **Nusa Penida** and **Nusa Lembongan** are popular with overnighters on Nusa Lembongan but also with daytrippers to both islands. Recommended is Crystal Divers (www.crystal-divers.com).

GOLF

Golfing opportunities abound, and courses are located throughout Java, among other islands. Die-hard duffers recommend the following for their challenges, views and facilities:

JAVA
Damai Indah Golf, Jakarta,
www.damaiindahgolf.com
Royale Jakarta Golf Club, Jakarta,
http://royalejakarta.com

BALI
New Kuta Golf Club, Pecatu,
http://newkutagolf.com

SUMATRA
Ria Bintan Golf Club, Bintan Island,
www.riabintan.com

KAYAKING

An exciting itinerary at **Komodo National Park** (page 23) includes land excursions, diving and snorkeling, and paddling from islet to islet while giving back to local communities and protecting the environment (No Roads Expeditions, www.noroads.com.au).

At **Raja Ampat** in western Papua, kayak with trained local guides, at the same time supporting native residents (Kayak4Conservation, www.kayak4conservation.com).

RAFTING

Although white-water rafting, tubing and bodyboarding are popular on almost every Indonesian river, the best areas are as follows and pass breathtaking scenery, waterfalls, rice fields and forests:

River rafting

Surfing

BALI

The Ayung and Telaga Waja Rivers, Class II–III, suitable for beginners all year (Sobek, http://balisobek.com; Bali Adventures (www.baliadventures.com)).

SUMATRA

Raft through Class II rapids on the Wampu River in Gunung Leuser National Park either with family-owned Tri Jaya Tour & Travel (www.trijaya-travel.com) or with Friendship Guesthouse (www.ketambe.com).

JAVA

In central Java near Borobudur, the Elo, Progo and Serayu Rivers range from Classes I to V depending on seasonal rainfall (Citra Elo Rafting, www.yogyes.com). Shoot the rapids on the Citarik River in Gunung Halimun-Salak National Park, Sukabumi, western Java, with Arusliar (http://arusliar.co.id).

Surfing

Indonesia's southern and western shores are nirvana for surfers, with the dry season (April–October) preferred in most areas. See www.surfing-waves.com for maps, videos, surf camps and loads of other information.

Favored waves for extreme surfers in

Bali, the epicenter of Indonesian surfing, are Uluwatu and Padang, with Kuta, the original Indonesian beach resort, ideal for beginners. On the southwest coast are Canggu, Balian and Medewi. In southwest **Lombok** is legendary Desert Point (Bangko-Bangko), with several choices on Kuta beach in the south. While **Java**'s biggest breaks are at G-Land, **Sumatra**'s favored surf spots are off Mentawi Island.

Sumbawa is known for Scar Reef, Super Suck and Yo-Yo's in the west, and world-class waves at Lakey beach. **Sumba**'s south coast presents challenges at Kerewe, Marosi and Dasang beaches, with one of Indonesia's top waves at Nihiwatu.

HIKES & ECO-TRIPS

Bird-watching

Indonesia, with its thousands of islands, has some of the world's best birding and there are ample opportunities for finding winged wonders in flight anywhere there are forests or water sources. Check www.burung.org for an excellent bird database.

In **western Java**, Pulau Dua and Pamojan Besar, near Banten, harbor hundreds of migratory birds. In addition

Photographing Mt Bromo, Java

to birds, **Maluku** is home to an astonishing array of butterflies and moths. Look for Australian and Wallace Line transition zone species at **Komodo National Park** (page 23) and primarily Asian species in **Sumatra** and **Kalimantan**. Two outfitters in Papua, home of the magnificent bird of paradise, offer specialized birdwatching tours (http://jefalgitours.com; www. bird-watching-papua-adventure-travel.com). In **central Bali**, Bali Bird Walks (http://balibirdwalk.com) is the best contact, and for a rare opportunity to see highly endangered free-ranging Bali starlings on Nusa Penida, visit www.fnpf.org.

Eco-tours

In **western Flores**, trek with local guides to villages, staying in their modest homes (Flores Exotic Tours, http://floresexotictours.com).

Travel in **Bali**, **Nusa Tenggara** and **Sulawesi** with Indonesia's leading textile experts, Threads of Life (www.threadsoflife.com), for a deeper appreciation of Indonesian cultures, or stroll in **Bali** with Keep Walking Tours (www.balispirit.com/tours). Trek through farms, villages and forests with a trained local guide or release hatchling turtles with JED (Jaringan Ekowisata Desa/Village Ecotourism Network, www.jed.or.id).

Walk through **Papua**'s gaspingly beautiful Baliem Valley (page 24), trek to see the Korowai treehouse people, or join an extreme hike to Lake Habema with Jefalgi Tours (http://jefalgitours.com). In eastern **Kalimantan**, visit remote Dayak villages with De'Gigant Tours, whose website (www.borneotourgigant.com) contains possibly the most complete information available for that part of the archipelago.

Volcano climbing/trekking & caving

Papua's glacier-topped **Puncak Jaya (Carstensz Pyramid)** is this country's most difficult climb, but finding an outfitter that leads expeditions is both challenging and expensive. For great information on Indonesia's tallest peaks, visit www.gunungbagging.com.

In **Lombok**, summiting Mt Rinjani requires an overnight en route, and as with most peaks it is closed to climbers during the rainy season (roughly November–March). The Rinjani Trekking Club (www.rinjanitrekking.com) provides information and guides (required).

Indonesia's second highest peak (after Puncak Jaya) is Mt Kerinci in western **Sumatra**. For this and other expeditions, visit Base Camp Adventure Shops (www.basecampindonesia.com). **Java**'s tallest mountain is Mt Semeru and is flanked by Mts Merapi and Merbabu, near Borobudur. See www.equator-indonesia.com for these treks and others as well as caving south of Jogja.

Climbs, treks & caves

For those who prefer getting involved during their holidays, several organizations offer volunteer opportunities as well as lodging and day trips for visitors.

BALI

Volunteering with **Side by Side Organic Farm** (https://sites.google.

com) is a great way to help impoverished villages in eastern Bali. Proceeds from hiking and biking tours, homestay programs and Balinese dance lessons help local communities.

JAVA

The Learning Farm (http://thelearningfarm.com) helps disadvantaged youth in western Java, near Puncak. Volunteers of all talents, including English language, arts and life skills, are welcome.

Habitat for Humanity (www.habitat-indonesia.org) is one of the many international aid organizations represented in Indonesia. It builds houses and clean water systems in natural disaster areas.

SULAWESI

Operation Wallacea (www.opwall.com) in Wakatobi, southeast Sulawesi, has programs for volunteer and student researchers.

In northern Sulawesi, the **Tasikoki Wildlife Rescue & Education Center** (www.tasikoki.org) accepts volunteers to care for animals rescued from the illegal wildlife trade. Day tours can be arranged through Wira Tours (www.sulawesi-celebes.com).

KALIMANTAN

The **Borneo Orangutan Survival Foundation**'s project in eastern Kalimantan focuses on reforestation, animal rehabilitation and community development. Its Samboja Lodge (www.sambojalodge.com) houses volunteers and tourists.

Wildlife-spotting

In addition to the famed Komodo dragons, there are many opportunities to track some of nature's wildest creatures,

particularly in national parks. Expert guides can be hired on the spot at the Forestry Department offices at **Ujung Kulon National Park**, western Java, and at **West Bali National Park**, with several choices of terrain and level of difficulty. Elephants are used to patrol park boundaries and perform in educational shows at **Way Kambas National Park**, southern Sumatra. Take a safari or river trip for wild game-spotting and excellent bird-watching. Also in the park is a Sumatran Rhino Sanctuary.

Safari Tours & Travel in Manado, northern Sulawesi (www.manadosafaris.com) offers treks through **Tangkoko Nature Reserve** and **Bogani Nani Wartabone National Park** in search of some of the island's many odd and endemic species, which are also found in **Lore Lindu National Park** (Wira Tours, www.sulawesi-celebes.com).

Borneo orangutans, as well as web-footed proboscis monkeys, are abundant at **Tanjung Puting National Park** in central Kalimantan (Thomas Wuwur, http://orangutanexotictours.com). Closely related Sumatran orangutans can be spotted at Bohorok in **Gunung Leuseur National Park**, where guides can be hired at the Forestry Department office or booked through Bukit Lawang Ecolodge (http://ecolodge.yelweb.org), operated by the Foundation for Sustainable Ecosystems.

Orangutans

BEST KID-FRIENDLY ACTIVITIES

Kids are welcome everywhere in this country, as all Indonesians love children. In addition to the activities listed here, check the websites of five-star resorts, as many have kids' clubs with a wide range of activities throughout the day.

JAKARTA & WEST JAVA

Ragunan Zoo, Beautiful Indonesia in Miniature Park (Taman Mini Indonesia Indah), Ancol Dreamland (Taman Impian Jaya Ancol), SeaWorld (http://seaworldindonesia.com) and the Thousand Islands (Kepulaun Seribu) are among Jakarta's best kid-friendly places.

In the Puncak Highlands, west Java, the Safari Park (Taman Safari) at Cipanas is a 168-ha (400-acre) recreational compound where wild animals forage in drive-through pastures in one area, and in the other area are kids' rides, food outlets and educational animal shows. Next door, factory tours at the Gunung Mas Tea Plantation show how tea leaves are sorted, processed and packaged. You can also tour the plantation on foot or horseback with a guide who explains tea cultivation.

On the opposite side of Mt Gede-Pangrango National Park is a canopy walk and a 'catwalk trail' at the Bodogol Conservation Education Center and Javan Gibbon Center, both with excellent chances of spotting some of the park's 245 bird species, leopards, Javan gibbons and grizzled leaf monkeys.

On Java's west coast, Java Sea Charters (http://javaseacharters.com) conducts PADI diving courses for ages eight years and above, cruises to the infamous Mt Krakatau, Ujung Kulon National Park and south Sumatra and co-sponsors an annual reef-building project in cooperation with the World Wildlife Fund.

CENTRAL JAVA

Ideal for a family island getaway, Karimunjawa Islands National Park is off the north coast of central Java. Its main attractions are gorgeous beaches, a treasure trove of marine life for snorkeling and diving, bird-watching and sun-worshiping. There are many budget homestays and a few hotels on the five inhabited islands. For luxury accommodations, Kura Kura Resort (www.kurakuraresort.com) offers guests use of sea kayaks, paddle boats and snorkeling equipment, as well as dolphin-spotting and sunset cruises and dive instructions for kids over eight.

BALI

One of the most kid-friendly beach destinations on Bali is Pemuteran on the northwest coast, where the waters are brimming with marine life and are calm enough for beginners to snorkel. In the same area and also nearby in West Bali National Park's Menjangan Island are challenging dives for the more experienced. Also check out the family-oriented resorts on Medewi beach on the south coast of western Bali.

Eastern Bali's Amed 14 km (8.7 mi.) stretch of beaches is also great for families; the countryside is dramatically rocky and the sea is crystal clear. In addition to snorkeling from the shore, hire a local fishing boat to go dolphin-watching or swimming in the sea, or watch the local people distilling salt from sea water. Not far away, at Tulamben, is the WW II shipwreck

Bali Bird Park

USAT Liberty, popular with wreck divers.

The first stop for many families on holiday in southern Bali is award-winning **Waterbom Bali** in Tuban, with a large enough variety of activities to keep everyone happy. For the kids (and the young at heart), there are water slides and rides and a supervised kids' area, and for everyone a bungy jump, spa treatments, reflexology, fish spa to relax aching feet, several food outlets and a sunken pool bar.

Bali Marine & Safari Park (www.balisafarimarinepark.com) on the southeast coast is understandably proud of its state-of-the-art concepts in zoo design that are both animal and visitor friendly. Educational animal shows are featured in this section. In another area, rides and a water park are sure to keep kids amused all day. The park theater's afternoon dance performances are a contemporary blend of culture, music and animals.

For seafaring families, nothing can compete with a sailing cruise, and there are several excellent options. **Bali Hai Cruises** (www.balihaicruises.com) participates in several conservation programs (sea turtle rescue, mangroves and reef restoration), and its options include day sails featuring parasailing, kayaking, water volleyball and banana boat rides; mangrove tours; and dolphin-spotting cruises. **Bounty Cruises** (www.balibountycruises.com) also has day cruises that focus on water sports as well as optional fly fishing. **Waka Experience** (www.wakaexperience.com) day cruises sail to its resort on Lembongan Island for water activities and up Bali's east coast. All three sail from Benoa Harbor and also offer dinner cruises.

Bali's animal parks can be educational or just plain fun. The **Elephant Safari Park** (www.baliadventures.com), north of Ubud, focuses on conservation and breeding of Sumatran elephants as well as public

education. Take a jungle safari on elephantback, visit the museum and information centers, and see performances designed to display pachyderm intelligence.

Arguably one of the best facilities of its kind anywhere, the **Bali Bird Park** (http://bali-bird-park.com), in Singapadu near Ubud, is divided into areas focusing on the tropical continents of the exotic birds found within: Latin America, South Africa and Indonesia, with each landscaped to resemble natural habitats. Have breakfast with the birds near the ibis pond, stroll through the free-flight aviary, and don't miss the impressive birds of paradise. Across the road from Bali Bird Park is **Rimba Reptile Park**, housing a large collection of snakes, turtles, lizards and Komodo dragons.

Treat your kids to an educational and fun experience at **Green Camp** (www.green-campbali.com), which has both day and overnight camps for kids that explore eco-living, sustainable agriculture, natural crafts and team-building. There are also family weekend and holiday programs.

Spend a day (or more) in a traditional Balinese housing compound experiencing a family's daily activities at **Taman Sari Buwana farming village** (http://bali-village.com) northwest of Ubud. Plow a field, plant rice, make offerings, cook over a wood-fueled fire, visit a school and sing songs with the kids, and go trekking through the fields to see farmers at work. This is a sustainable tourism project that is both educational and fun for everyone.

INDONESIA'S BEST TEMPLES & MUSEUMS

JAKARTA

Apart from the 15 museums in **Beautiful Indonesia in Miniature** (Taman Mini Indonesia Indah), Jakarta's best antiquities collections are housed in colonial-era buildings in Old Town (page 11) and in the Sudirman/Thamrin business district (page 12). Visit www.heritagejkt.org for free tours in several languages of the **National Museum** (Museum Nasional).

Formerly the home of a 19th-century Frenchman, the **Textile Museum** (Museum Tekstil, http://museumtekstil-jakarta.com) contains nearly 2,000 woven, non-woven, batik and contemporary cloths, which are displayed on a rotating basis. The bonus is its workshop where, for a small fee, you can create your own batik masterpiece.

CENTRAL JAVA

Upon arrival, the vast majority of Jogja's visitors head straight to monumental **Borobudur** (page 15). **Prambanan** and the **Roro Jonggrang Plains temples** are east of Jogja (page 43).

From Borobodur, some continue north to **Dieng Plateau** but very few make the time to wander uphill to breathtaking **Gedong Songo** or make a side trip to the **Railway Museum** at Ambarawa.

In Jogja, the royal regalia museums are included in every **Sultan's Palace** (Keraton) tour (page 14), and visions of days gone by are at **Taman Sari 'Water Castle'**, **Kota Gede** and **Imogiri** (pages 41–3). South of town in a rural village, **Tembi Rumah Budaya**, is a highly active cultural center dedicated to the study of classical Javanese culture. Its compound includes a museum, exhibition and art studio spaces and accommodations in restored Javanese teak houses.

North of Jogja in Kaliurang, a strangely out of place European-style castle peeks from behind an overgrowth of vegetation. This is **Museum Ullen Sentalu** (http://ullensentalu.com), owned by a member of a Javanese royal family, that houses an excellent collection of antiquities.

East of Jogja, near Solo, on the slopes of sacred Mt Lawu, are two very distinctive temples believed to have been erected in the 15th century at the end of the Majapahit empire. **Candi Sukuh** is a flat-topped pyramid resembling a Mayan monument, its statues and reliefs featuring male and female genitals seemingly symbolizing rebirth. Like Candi Sukuh, **Candi Ceto** is dedicated to Bima and also features phallic symbols. Why the architecture and icons of both temples deviate so greatly from all other Javanese monuments remains a mystery.

Nearby is Sangiran, a UNESCO World Heritage Site where the fossils of 'Java Man' (*Homo erectus*) were discovered. The **Sangiran Site Museum** contains replicas of the Java Man skull pieces, artifacts and other fossils, some dating back 1.5 million years.

EAST JAVA

The trail of the ancient Javanese kingdoms extends to eastern Java, where political power shifted after central Java's Mataram kingdom fell in the 10th century. Archaeologists dig in this region at a fevered pace, hopeful of unraveling more of Java's mysterious past.

Candi Badut (*candi* is Indonesian for 'temple') (page 46), now almost completely encompassed by Malang city, is eastern Java's oldest surviving Hindu temple, constructed in the mid-700s AD. Outside of the city are 13th-century **Candi Kidal**, **Candi Jago** and **Candi Singosari**. **Candi Jawi** and the older **Candi Pari** are to the north (see page 46).

South of Mojokerto is **Trowulan**, which is believed to have been the site of once-magnificent Majapahit's ancient city. Most of the structures have returned to dust, but there is a Site Museum. Near Kediri are the unfinished 14th-century **Candi Surowono** and the relief-encircled base of **Candi Tegurwangi**.

Continuing south, at Tulungagung, are the remains of **Candi Boyolangu** and **Candi Cungkup**, but more interesting are 10th-century **Gua Selamangleng** and **Gua Pasir**, meditation caves decorated with bas reliefs. Rounding out the antiquities tour, near Blitar are the ruins of small **Candi Simpang** and the remains of an impressive complex, **Candi Panataran**.

BALI

In the 16th century, Javanese Majapahit high priest Danghyang Niratha fled to Bali to escape encroaching Islamic empires and established seven coastal sea temples in areas where he stopped to meditate. **Pura Tanah Lot**, the 'Temple of the Earth in the Sea' (page 50), is perched atop a large, rocky outcrop off the southwestern coast near Canggu. It is also one of the *sad kahyangan* temples meant to unite all Hindu-Balinese, each of which is consecrated to significant features of the landscape: forest, mountains, sea, lakes, earth and rice fields. Foreigners may not enter the temple, but its pagoda-shaped roof (*meru*) takes on a magnificent aura at sunset.

Another of the *sad kahyangan* and also a sea temple is **Pura Luhur Ulu Watu** on the west coast of the island's southernmost peninsula (page 51). Originally built in the 11th century, it was reconstructed in the 16th century by Niratha, who is said to have attained *moksa* (release from earthly desires) here. Visitors may tour the compound but the innermost sanctuary is open only to those who wish to pray.

Resting on outcroppings jutting out into a recreational lake, somehow managing to retain its dignity, is **Pura Ulun Danu Bratan** in the Bedugal Highlands of central Bali. It was built in the 17th century by a Mengwi king and is dedicated to the lake goddess, Dewi Danu, who is much revered as a source of fertility. The main shrine, with an 11-tiered *meru* roof, is dedicated to Wisnu in his manifestation as Dewi Danu, who protects all living creatures.

The most sacred and powerful of all of Bali's many temples and a major locus of divine power in the Bali-Hindu cosmos is **Pura Besakih**, a large complex often referred to as the 'Mother Temple' (page 58). Twenty-two temples are spread along a distance of more than a kilometer. On the outskirts of the compound, which was established as early as the 8th century, are dozens of ancestral and public temples and hundreds of shrines, which were added later.

Bali's most-visited ancient sites include the 11th-century **Elephant Cave** (Goa Gajah) (page 53) and nearby bronze kettledrum **Moon of Pejeng** (300 BC). In eastern Bali are the 17th-century **Kertha Gosa Hall of Justice** and the **Floating Pavilion** (Balé Kambang) in Semarapura (pages 56-7), and one of Bali's last remaining pre-Hindu *Bali Aga* villages, **Tenganan** (page 57).

TRAVEL FACTS

Downtown Jakarta at night

Local transportation

Parangtritis beach, Yogyakarta

Visas

Visitors from the following 12 countries are allowed a non-extendable 30-day visa free of charge upon arrival in Indonesia: Brunei, Chile, Ecuador, Hong Kong SAR, Macau SAR, Malaysia, Morocco, Peru, the Philippines, Singapore, Thailand and Vietnam.

Visa on arrival (VOA) regulations are forever in a state of flux, but currently citizens of 65 countries (see www.kemlu. go.id for the latest listing) can obtain a 30-day visa upon entering the country by paying a US$25 fee. This visa can be extended for 30 days at the immigration office in major cities.

Those from all other countries must apply for a visa at an Indonesian embassy or consulate prior to arrival.

All passports must be valid for a minimum of six months, and some immigration offices require at least six blank passport pages. You must also have an air ticket exiting Indonesia.

Booking a Flight

Airports throughout the country are being upgraded and new ones built to accommodate more passengers, and airlines and flight schedules change at a rapid pace. Booking with a reputable local travel agent is a good idea, particularly for in-country travel. The best Indonesian travel agencies have reservations websites for transportation, accommodations and multilingual guides, saving you time and energy on arrival. Highly recommended is **KCBJ Tours & Travel Services** (www.kcbtours.com) in Bali. There are also small agencies in almost every city and town that sell train, bus and air tickets that will have the latest schedules. In larger hotels, the travel desk is usually manned by a travel agency representative.

International Airports

The two major entry points into Indonesia are Jakarta's **Sukarno-Hatta International Airport** and Bali's **Ngurah Rai International Airport** near Denpasar. However, most islands have at least one airport, and often more, that cater to carriers such as AirAsia, Malaysia Airlines, Lion Air, Tiger Airways and Silk Air arriving from other Asian cities (see 'Booking a Flight' above).

Arriving

The first matter to attend to is the visa checkpoint if arriving on an international flight (see 'Visas' above) followed by Customs clearance. Forbidden are narcotics (a very serious offence, the possession of which can be punishable by death), arms and ammunition, pornography, fresh fruit, the import or export of Indonesian currency exceeding Rp5 million, and products made from endangered species. There is no restriction on the import or export of foreign currencies. Allowed are 1 liter of alcoholic beverage, 200 cigarettes (or 50 cigars or 100 g of tobacco) and a reasonable quantity of perfume per adult.

Getting Around in Jakarta

After exiting the baggage claim area in the Jakarta international terminal, taxi companies each have their own queues serviced by a dispatcher who will help you load luggage. Be advised there is a surcharge that is in addition to the metered fare. Avoid the touts offering transport en route to the taxi areas. **Blue Bird Taxi** and its affiliate companies (such as **Pusaka**) have the best safety and courtesy records. Also recommended is **Express**. **Silver Bird** is Blue Bird's executive version. It costs more but is worth it in comfort if you have money to spare. In the city, if you hail a taxi on the street and the driver refuses to turn on the meter, get out and find another taxi.

In Jakarta proper there are several varieties of buses for getting around town, but the handiest is the **Transjakarta** 'busway', that shuttles thousands of people to and fro every day. A route map can be downloaded at www.rutebusway.com. Word to the wise: Delay busway rides until after about 9 am and before around 4 pm on weekdays in order to avoid the hordes of people trying to get to or from work.

Getting Around Indonesia
At the Bali international terminal, you pay at the **taxi** counter just outside the baggage claim area where rates to various destinations are posted on a board. You'll receive a receipt containing the taxi number, then join a queue to wait for yours to arrive.

For **flights** to other domestic destinations, see 'Booking a Flight' above.

Throughout Java and Bali there are **buses** of varying levels of cost and comfort shuttling masses of people from one place to another each day. For air-conditioned comfort, check with a local travel agent for schedules and prices for 'express', 'first class' or 'executive class' service to your destination. **Perama Tours** has an extensive network of bus routes in Java, Bali, Lombok and Flores and has a good reputation for safety and efficiency. Check local offices for schedules.

Java is the only island with an extensive **rail** system, with east-west service. Executive class is definitely worth the extra cost. Get schedules and book your passage from local travel agents at least two days in advance. Otherwise, show up at the station one hour or more before scheduled departure to purchase tickets.

Car Rentals & Driving
Avis and **Hertz** have offices in Jakarta, but there are also many large locally owned car rental companies, such as **Bluebird/**

Golden Bird (www.bluebirdbroup.com) in Jakarta and Bali and **Autobagus Rent a Car** (www.autobagus.com) in Bali, as well as many small companies.

Self-driving requires an international driver's license and is not recommended due to road conditions, traffic and unexpected occurrences, such as people and animals crossing roads. It's far better to hire a car or minivan with a driver and leave the worrying to him. Some companies will include an English-speaking guide for an extra charge who can be a bonus if he understands what type of experience you're after. On day trips, it is customary to pay for the driver and guide's meals and snacks, and also for their accommodations if staying overnight.

In tourist areas, particularly in Bali, men often stand on the main roads shouting 'transport' and some of them are very good. However, check the condition of the vehicle, discuss your itinerary and negotiate a price before consenting to hire anyone. Car and driver rentals can also be arranged through most accommodations, even modest ones.

Serviced Apartments
There are several options for serviced apartments in Jakarta, such as The Ascott (www.the-ascott.com) and The Mayflower (www.marriott.com). On Bali, do a web search for 'villas for rent' to find a mind-boggling list of options. Most come with a maid and often a cook and a driver. Also check Harris Hotel & Residences Riverview Kuta (http://harrishotels.com), as well as hotels in southern Bali with kitchenettes.

Money Matters
Indonesian currency is rupiah (Rp) and notes come in Rp100,000, Rp50,000, Rp20,000, Rp10,000, Rp5,000, Rp2,000 and Rp1,000 denominations. Coins are Rp100, 500 and 1,000, with a few old Rp50 still floating around.

Banks operate 8–9 am until 4–5 pm Monday–Friday. ATMs accepting major credit cards and international ATM cards for cash withdrawals are abundant in major cities. Off-the-beaten path, it's advisable to take what cash you think you'll need. Note that most ATMs limit total amounts withdrawn per machine and many cards have cash withdrawal limits in a 24-hour period, so plan carefully. Keep a good supply of small denomination notes at all times, as larger ones, particularly Rp100,000, can be difficult to break.

Moneychangers usually have a better exchange rate than banks or hotels, and the most reliable ones are found at the Jakarta and Bali airports. On the streets, moneychangers post exchange rates on boards. Choose one that says it is 'Authorized', and beware of rates that look too good to be true, particularly around Kuta in Bali, where scams are prevalent.

Visa and MasterCard are the most widely accepted credit cards in larger shops and hotels, though American Express and Diner's Club are also taken in some places. Many locally owned shops will add a 3–5 percent service charge, which is an accepted practice.

Keep a stash of cash tucked away for your international departure tax when leaving the country, which must be paid in rupiah. Fees vary from region to region and frequently change, but currently are Rp150,000 from both Jakarta and Bali.

Tipping

In local eating establishments away from tourist areas, tips are not expected. However, where tourists have tipped in the past, it has become the custom to tip between 5 and 10 percent. Large hotels and upscale restaurants usually add a 10 percent 'service charge' to cover tips, which is distributed among all the staff.

For taxis and hired cars, tipping is not mandatory but is a nice thing to do if the service was good. Round up to the nearest Rp1,000 on the meter for taxis; for rental cars, the driver will appreciate Rp20,000–50-000 for a day's outing. Double that amount for the guide.

Airport and hotel porters will smile at Rp10,000 per piece for regular luggage and a bit more for heavy or bulky items.

Tips in rupiah are best.

Useful Websites & Tourist Police

On the whole, government-operated **tourism information** offices and websites are woefully lacking in useful information. Many travel agencies have websites, although the bulk of them are not kept current. Check copyright dates on websites before relying on cyber-info. Many of the best tourist information websites have already been mentioned elsewhere in this book. Below are a few more:

- Bali: www.bali-travel-life.com
- Java: www.ujungkulon-tour.com; www.eastjava.com; www.houseofsampoerna.museum; www.jogjapages.com; www.yogyes.com
- Kalimantan: www.kalimantantours.com; www.extremeborneo.com
- Maluku: www.divingmaluku.com
- Nusa Tenggara: http://florestourism.com; www.lavalontouristinfo.com; www.kupangklubhouse.com
- Sulawesi: www.north-sulawesi.org
- Sumatra: http://toursumatra.com

Jakarta and southern Bali both have **Tourist Police** who wear special uniforms, speak English and patrol popular areas. Visitors are encouraged to approach these men and women with any questions or concerns. Kuta has a new Tourist Police Gallery with displays of police equipment, a small library and free WiFi.

Calendar of Events

The dates of many Indonesian public holidays change every year as they are determined by phases of the moon rather than the Gregorian calendar. The dates below, in most cases, are approximate:

New Year's Day — January 1
Chinese New Year — January
Birthday of the Prophet
    Mohammad — February
Nyepi (Hindu New Year) — March
Good Friday — April
Waisak Day (Buddha's birth, enlightenment and death) — May
Ascension of Christ — May
Ascension of the Prophet
    Mohammad — June
Indonesian Independence Day —
    August 17
Idul Fitri (end of Ramadan) — August
Idul Adha (Muslim day of sacrifice) —
    October
Islamic New Year — November
Christmas Day — December 25

Ramadan, the Muslim fasting month, begins around July and for 30 days millions of Indonesians refrain from eating or drinking from sunup until sundown. Outside of primarily Hindu Bali, cafes and restaurants catering to tourists, particularly in hotels, remain open but usually curtain their windows out of respect to those fasting. Nightlife may be limited to hotels.

Throughout Indonesia, in the days leading up to **Indonesian Independence Day** (August 17), there are games, competitions and festivities everywhere, and the same is true for **Chinese New Year** (January). Ask at your accommodation if there are any special celebrations in the area if you visit during these times.

On Bali, **Nyepi** is a day of silence for 24 hours, beginning at sunrise. The airport is closed, no vehicles operate and no electricity is used except in hotels. On the eve of Nyepi there are grand processions, and offerings are made throughout the island to expel demons.

There are many other festivals held throughout the archipelago, for example, the **Bau Nyale** in Lombok, **Erau** in Kalimantan, **Pasola** in Sumba, **Reba** in Flores and a grand gathering of Buddhists from throughout the world at Borobudur on **Waisak Day**. In the sports arena is the **Raja Ampat Marine Festival** (Papua, May), **Indonesian Surfing Championship** (Seminyak, Bali, June) and the **Darwin-Ambon Yacht Race** with several stops in Indonesia (July–August), to name a few. Inquire upon arrival if any are being held during your visit. In Jakarta, look for film, fashion and jazz festivals, and on Bali, the **Bali Arts Festival** (http://baliartsfestival.com).

Climate & Seasons

The 'rainy season' lasts from November through March in the western part of the country, with a shorter period in the eastern islands. Rains rarely last all day; rather there may be heavy downpours for an hour or two followed by high humidity. The dry season is roughly April–October. Year round temperatures range from 21–33 °C (70–90 °F) in the flatlands and can be substantially cooler at higher altitudes.

Electricity

Electricity is usually 220V–240V AC. Power outages are common and voltages fluctuate, making using stabilizers advisable. Wall plugs are the Western European type with two round pins.

Mobile Phones & Internet

Indonesia's mobile phone (called 'handphone' here) service is three-band GSM. If your service provider does not offer international roaming, inexpensive cellular phones can be purchased here with prepaid SIM cards of varying denominations.

WiFi 'hotspots' are widely available in larger cities at cafes and shopping malls. If you are laptop or smartphone-free, look for 'internet cafes', full-service computer rental centers that charge by the hour and include Skype. Ask around for one with a high-speed connection; otherwise, be prepared to be patient.

Telephone Numbers

It is not unusual to see telephone numbers with as few as six or as many as eight digits, as telecommunications systems continue to expand. Phone numbers beginning with 08 are cellular phones and are used by both businesses and individuals.

Indonesia's country code is 62 and is followed by an area code. In-country, the country code is dropped and the area code is preceded by a zero. For example, if calling Jakarta (area code 21) from another country, dial 62-21 and the telephone number. However, if calling Jakarta from within Indonesia, dial 021 plus the phone number.

To call countries abroad when in Indonesia, you must first access one of the international operators by dialing 001 or 008, followed by the country code of the area you're calling, followed by the area code, and finally the telephone number. There are several other international access lines, but they have limited range and service.

For local directory assistance, dial 108; for an operator-assisted call, dial 101. An increasing number of operators speak English. For anything more sophisticated than this, visit the local Telkom office, the government-owned telecommunications company. (See also 'Mobile Phones & Internet' above.)

Emergency Telephone Numbers

In large cities, the following emergency telephone numbers can be used but be aware that traffic can cause delays in responding. In the case of medical emergencies, it might be quicker to flag down a taxi and head for the nearest hospital or clinic.

Ambulance—dial 118
Fire brigade—dial 113
Police—dial 112

Hospitals & Dentists

There are several pharmacy (*apotik*) franchises in major cities that operate 24/7, such as **Apotik K-24**. Others, such as **Guardian** and **Century**, are located in shopping malls, and there are literally hundreds of small locally owned *apotik*. If you don't find what you're looking for at one of them, try another.

In Jakarta, most expatriates rely on **SOS Medika Klinik Cipete** (Jl. Puri Sakti No. 10, Cipete, south Jakarta, Appointments Tel: (021) 750-5980; 24-hour Emergency Tel: (021) 750-6001) or its sister clinic **SOS Medika Klinik Kuningan** (Menara Prima 2nd Floor, Jl. Lingkar Mega Kuningan Blok 6.2, north Jakarta, Tel: (021) 5794-8600, www.sosindonesia.com for both). These two clinics offer general care, diagnostics and dental; the Cipete branch has an ambulance service and emergency evacuation capabilities.

On Bali, there are three international-standard facilities that provide a wide range of services:

BIMC HOSPITAL BALI: Kuta: Jl. Bypass Ngurah Rai No. 100X, Tel: (0361) 761-263.

BIMC HOSPITAL BALI: Nusa Dua: Kawasan BTDC Blok D, Tel: (0361) 300-0911 (www.bimcbali.com for both). General and 24-hour emergency care; can also facilitate emergency evacuation. Dentistry available at the Nusa Dua hospital.

SOS MEDIKA KLINIK BALI, KUTA: (Jl. Bypass Ngurah Rai No. 505X, Kuta. Appointments Tel: (0361) 720-100; 24-hour Emergency Tel: (0361) 710-505, www.sosindonesia.com). General and

24-hour emergency care; specialist services, including psychological; ambulance service; emergency evacuation capabilities.

Before leaving home, it is highly recommended that you acquire travel health insurance. In the remote event that the medical care you need is not available in Indonesia and you have to be evacuated to another country, charter transportation costs alone can run into thousands of dollars and must be paid in advance. International policies usually provide for these costs to be paid swiftly. While you're at it, also take out policies that cover lost luggage and canceled or delayed flights. The costs are negligible compared to the inconvenience caused in the event one of these policies needs to be put into play.

Embassies in Indonesia

Embassies representing the major countries and several minor ones are located in Jakarta, and there are 20 or so consulates in Bali. There are also a few consulates in Jogja and Surabaya (Java) and in Medan (Sumatra). Check the website of the country you're interested in for locations. Some of the major embassies in Jakarta are:

Jakarta

(all telephone numbers are area code 021)

AUSTRALIA: Jl. H.R. Rasuna Said Kav. 15-16, Tel: 2550-5555, www.indonesia.embassy.gov.au

BRITISH: Jl. M.H. Thamrin 75, Tel: 2356-5200, www.fco.gov.uk

JAPAN: Jl. M.H. Thamrin 24, Tel: 3192-4303, www.id.emb-japan.go.jp

MALAYSIA: Jl. H.R. Rasuna Said Kav X16, No. 1-3, Kuningan, Tel: 522-4947, http://malaysia.visahq.com

NETHERLANDS: Jl. H.R. Rasuna Said Kav S-3, Tel: 524-8200, http://indonesia.nlembassy.org

SINGAPORE: Jl. H.R. Rasuna Said Blok X-4 Kav. No. 2, Kuningan, Tel: 2995-0400, www.mfa.gov.sg

THAILAND: Jl. Imam Bonjol, Tel: 390-4052, http://thailand.visahq.com

UNITED STATES: Jl. Medan Merdeka Selatan No. 3-5, Jakarta, Tel: 3435-9000, http://jakarta.usembassy.gov

Opening Hours

Government offices usually open at 8 am, closing Monday–Thursday 3 pm, Friday 11.30 am, Saturday 2 pm, and some close for lunch. Visit them in the mornings to be safe, and be sure to dress appropriately (no beachwear or flop-flops). Most businesses operate from 8–9 am until 4–5 pm Monday–Friday. Shops open at 9 or 10 am, depending on location, and stay open until 9 or 10 pm, but those outside of shopping malls may close at noon for *istirahat* (rest time). Government-owned museums are closed on Mondays.

Postal & Shipping Services

Post offices (*kantor pos*) are generally open the same hours as other government agencies (see 'Opening Hours' above), and they provide several services in addition to selling stamps, such as Western Union. They accept packages up to 20 kg (44 lb). FedEx, UPS and many other international courier services, as well as local ones, also operate in Indonesia.

Shops selling furniture, art and larger items for export usually have relationships with cargo services that will wrap, fumigate and otherwise prepare and ship your purchases.

Safety & Security

Most Indonesians are honest people, but particularly in large cities or tourist locations problems can occur. Beware of pickpockets in crowds, store your valuables in safety deposit boxes in rooms or at the front desks of smaller hotels, lock rental cars and keep personal possessions out of sight, and make sure luggage is locked before arriving at airports.

Health issues include dehydration, upset stomach and diarrhea, dengue fever, malaria, Hepatitis A, B and E and a growing number of HIV cases. Take the usual precautions.

Food Safety

All water should be made safe before drinking; bottled water is available almost everywhere. Some restaurants and hotels serve drinking water in pitchers or Thermos containers. If the water is hot, it has been boiled. If it's cold, inquire if it came from a 'gallon', meaning a large jug of bottled water.

In general, salads, fruits, ice and water served at up-end hotels and restaurants are safe to consume, as their reputations are at stake. Outside these establishments eat only cooked foods and fruits you peel yourself, skip salads and drink bottled water. Beware of street food or that in small *warung* (eateries), which have lax cleanliness and food storage standards.

Basic Survival Indonesian
CIVILITIES

Welcome *Selamat datang*
Good morning (7-11 am) *Selamat pagi*
Good midday (11 am-3 pm) *Selamat siang*
Good afternoon (3-7 pm) *Selamat sore*
Goodnight (after dark) *Selamat malam*
Goodbye (to one leaving) *Selamat jalan*
Goodbye (to one staying) *Selamat tinggal*
Thank you *Terima kasih*
You're welcome *Kembali*

NUMBERS

1 *satu*	6 *enam*
2 *dua*	7 *tujuh*
3 *tiga*	8 *delapan*
4 *empat*	9 *sembilan*
5 *lima*	10 *sepuluh*

DIRECTIONS

north *utara*	outside *di luar*
south *selatan*	left *kiri*
east *timur*	right *kanan*
west *barat*	near *dekat*
inside *di dalam*	far *jauh*

TIME

minute *menit*	later *nanti*
hour *jam* (also	Sunday *Hari Minggu*
clock/watch)	Monday *Hari Senin*
day *hari*	Tuesday *Hari Selasa*
week *minggu*	Wednesday *Hari*
month *bulan*	*Rabu*
year *tahun*	Thursday *Hari*
today *hari ini*	*Kamis*
tomorrow *besok*	Friday *Hari Jumat*
yesterday *kemarin*	Saturday *Hari Sabtu*

Etiquette & Taboos

In predominantly Muslim regions, it is impolite to give or receive anything with the left hand, which is considered dirty. Particularly in villages, which are generally more conservative, women should have their knees and armpits covered and men should wear shirts with sleeves (no tank tops). Public displays of affection are frowned upon.

On Bali, sarongs or sashes are required in temples and are available for a small donation before entering temples. Swimsuits should not be worn away from beaches.

Everywhere: Address elders as *Bapak* or *Pak* (Mr) and *Ibu* or *Bu* (Mrs) to show respect. Remove shoes before entering someone's house or a place of worship. It is not polite to photograph people's faces while they are praying.

INDEX

PHOTO CREDITS

The Tuttle Story: "Books to Span the East and West"

Many people are surprised when they learn that the world's largest publisher of books on Asia had its humble beginnings in the tiny American state of Vermont. The company's founder, Charles Tuttle, came from a New England family steeped in publishing.

Tuttle's father was a noted antiquarian dealer in Rutland, Vermont. Young Tuttle honed his knowledge of the trade working in the family bookstore, and later in the rare books section of Columbia University Library. His passion for beautiful books—old and new—never wavered through his long career as a bookseller and publisher.

After graduating from Harvard, Tuttle enlisted in the military and in 1945 was sent to Tokyo to work on General Douglas MacArthur's staff. He was tasked with helping to revive the Japanese publishing industry, which had been utterly devastated by the war. When his tour of duty was completed, he left the military, married a talented and beautiful singer, Reiko Chiba, and in 1948 began several successful business ventures.

To his astonishment, Tuttle discovered that postwar Tokyo was actually a book-lover's paradise. He befriended dealers in the Kanda district and began supplying rare Japanese editions to American libraries. He also imported American books to sell to the thousands of GIs stationed in Japan. By 1949, Tuttle's business was thriving, and he opened Tokyo's very first English-language bookstore in the Takashimaya Department Store in Ginza, to great success. Two years later, he began publishing books to fulfill the growing interest of foreigners in all things Asian.

Though a westerner, Tuttle was hugely instrumental in bringing a knowledge of Japan and Asia to a world hungry for information about the East. By the time of his death in 1993, he had published over 6,000 books on Asian culture, history and art—a legacy honored by Emperor Hirohito in 1983 with the "Order of the Sacred Treasure," the highest honor Japan can bestow upon a non-Japanese.

The Tuttle company today maintains an active backlist of some 1,500 titles, many of which have been continuously in print since the 1950s and 1960s—a great testament to Charles Tuttle's skill as a publisher. More than 60 years after its founding, Tuttle Publishing is more active today than at any time in its history, still inspired by Charles Tuttle's core mission—to publish fine books to span the East and West and provide a greater understanding of each.

Also available from Tuttle Publishing/Periplus Editions
www.tuttlepublishing.com

ISBN 978-0-8048-4260-0

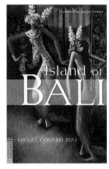

ISBN 978-7946-0-562-9

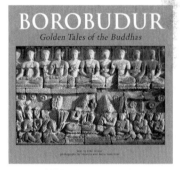

ISBN 978-0-945971-90-0

ISBN 978-0-8048-3776-7

ISBN 978-0-8048-3896-2

ISBN 978-0-8048-4183-2

ISBN 978-0-8048-4246-4

ISBN 978-0-8048-4198-6

ISBN 978-0-8048-4145-0